ALSO BY ANI GJIKA

POETRY

Bread on Running Waters

TRANSLATIONS

Negative Space, by Luljeta Lleshanaku
Memories Pretend to Sleep, by Julia Gjika
Emergency Exit, by Xhevdet Bajraj
We Fall Like Children, by Xhevdet Bajraj
Slaying the Mosquito, by Xhevdet Bajraj
A Poem of Love, by Lisandri Kola

ANI GJIKA

AN
UNRULED
BODY

A Poet's Memoir

RESTLESS BOOKS

NEW YORK · AMHERST

This book is a work of creative nonfiction.
Some names and identifying details have been changed.

Copyright © 2023 Ani Gjika

Excerpted poems from *Bread on Running Waters*, copyright
© 2013 Ani Gjika. Reprinted by permission of Fenway Press.

All rights reserved.

Restless Books and the R colophon are registered trademarks of Restless Books, Inc.

First Restless Books hardcover edition November 2023

Hardcover ISBN: 9781632063403
Library of Congress Control Number: 2023939500

This book is supported in part by an award from the National Endowment for the Arts.

This book is made possible by the New York State Council on the Arts with the
support of Governor Kathy Hochul and the New York State Legislature.

Cover design by Sarah Schulte
Set in Garibaldi by Tetragon, London

Printed in the United States of America

1 3 5 7 9 10 8 6 4 2

RESTLESS BOOKS
NEW YORK · AMHERST
www.restlessbooks.org

For my parents, for Anita Hoffer, and for Rebecca Loudon,
who once wished for me a desire to engage
in deep play in my art.

When we are young, the words are scattered all around us.
As they are assembled by experience, so also are we,
sentence by sentence, until the story takes shape.

LOUISE ERDRICH,
THE PLAGUE OF DOVES

CONTENTS

Prologue   3

PART ONE

How to Love   11
In India There's a Name for You   50
Girlhood   74
The Half-Lit Corner   94
Out of the Layers   117

PART TWO

All the Languages a Girl Carries   135
Crossing Over   152
Shooting Stars   165
Desire   189
I Have a Mouth   219
Atdhe: Home   231

Epilogue   249
Acknowledgments   255

AN
UNRULED
BODY

PROLOGUE

I AM HERE, IN MY CAR, ALONE. Driving home from an employee Christmas party to Ishan, the man I married six and a half years ago, who told me on Thanksgiving morning that he's leaving me. At this very moment, I feel pure joy, though not the kind that makes you worry the evil eye might get you, not tonight, and not at all in the years that will follow, when I allow joy to enter my body, my home.

I am driving on Main Street, suddenly very aware of how the layers of my clothes fit. I am wearing a black, unbuttoned A-shaped coat and underneath it a tight, peacock blue-green shirt over a long copper satin skirt. My curls are doing that shiny-no-frizz thing they do only once a week, kissing my shoulders and framing my face as if they're offering it. I am particularly enjoying the way my skirt feels against my skin, against my free, silky-smooth legs.

Driving through an intersection, I have the urge to open my legs and when I do, I feel an unlocking. I can't close them. I already know that I won't. I feel pleasantly dizzy and think, I shouldn't do this. It's not safe. But the thought flashes away faster than the people and cars I'm passing. I put one hand on my lap and begin lifting the cloth toward my belly, feeling charged, charging with every inch of movement I'm now causing.

It doesn't take long before I let my finger enter, then slip out, and enter again. First one finger, then two. My hand seems to know this new way of finding me, of finding how to touch so that each time is new and keeps changing my breathing. And if people see me? The thought briefly intercedes. But I feel such pleasure from the fact that I'm doing this now, driving in public, that no one is watching yet they could so easily discover me if they only looked. I am moaning. When my fingers no longer trace circles on my vulva or within the opening, when they thrust in and out now, finding their rhythm, I stop breathing and I'm so wet, for a moment I wonder where I'll wipe this hand. With each stroke and thrust I grow softer, wetter, wider. I have become an opening, all the layers of inhibition, fears, anxiety, insecurities I'd wrapped myself in for years shed from me, dissolved, the way you know pain only while going through it; afterward, the memory of it is mercurial—did it really exist? I am the lake after a stone falls in; with each thrust another ripple widens, bigger than the previous, and I'm rippling out, and out. I feel multiplied and distinctly singular at once. I am here in my car and dispersed through the universe at the same time. My throat is dry.

When I'm a child, my father finds me in daycare one afternoon sitting on a chair behind the door, mouth full of peas. Not swallowing them, not spitting them out. The daycare worker had started to feed me, but I don't like peas and won't have

4

them, so she punished me by making me sit behind the door after she force-fed a couple of spoonfuls. I am three years old and I know I've done something wrong. But I like to believe I am punishing her right back, in my own way, by holding a mouthful of peas, cheeks swollen, determined not to swallow until the world ends.

It will take decades for me to be this resolute again. When my body will learn to control my actions. But I don't know that now.

My mother brags that I've been strong-willed since I was young. But when my father, the storyteller, talks about this day, he often praises my ability to endure. "Oh, Ani," he says, "there's no one like her, she's the most patient. Have I told you about the time I went to pick her up from daycare and found her . . . ?" Laughing, the way only someone who means well laughs. But I don't agree.

This isn't a story about endurance. This is a story about listening to the language of my body. How I learned to listen to remember all that I am.

In Albania, language finds me before I can read. For years, I listen to my grandmother's stories from the Old Testament and recite the nursery rhymes she teaches me. Aside from a few days I spend at daycare, I play indoors and out-

Before writing, before toys, I used to draw stars. Mami sat knitting me a sweater, advising from time to time how to make an angle.

side in the neighborhood until I begin to attend public school in first grade. For the first six years of my life, I listen and absorb

5

the language of what surrounds me—books, grown-ups, dirt, nature, parades, my mother ironing clothes on Sundays. Language finds me again after I turn seven, the day Enver Hoxha dies. I write poetry to make sense of the Albanian tyrant's death. But I lose it in the years that follow when my country suffers the tragedies that accumulate when one system is toppled and everyone waits, dreaming of something better to take the old one's place. From the vantage of my eleven- or twelve-year-old eyes, it seems as though my country, determined to change itself overnight, has become a bullet train that derails and lands in a swamp, the engine pistons slowly but inevitably coming to a halt. I watch from a distance, the way young girls watch without speaking when the shape of their body is a threat to their own existence. It will take years for me to find language again, no longer my mother tongue but the language of America, the country in which my family and I will eventually arrive, the language I will later embrace as a writer and a translator.

I begin writing one April day my sophomore year in college, two years after immigrating to America. Maybe I have a crush on Ben, the son of family friends who live nearby, and maybe I have fallen in love with the poetry I read as a newly declared English major, but I grab a notebook and a pen, sit by the fire stairs of the house my family and I are living in, and write the whole afternoon, thirty little poems. This happens to me rarely—the flood of having something to say and the immediate need to write it down—but I trust it when it comes.

Later, as I move from one continent to another, from one language to another, writing becomes my only way home. All the emotions and stories I carry exist outside language, in my body, where they live. I am more at home on the page than when I speak English or Albanian. There is always a disconnect, the sense that someone will know the misfit I am as soon as I open my mouth. But when I'm writing, I'm sailing on a small boat at dusk in the middle of a lake—so much has quieted, the birds, the sunlight, the people who have walked back into their houses, and so much of what is absent begins to resound and ripple around the little boat. Everything I write comes from this heart space and seeks to give itself, to be shared. There is no critical voice, only the sense of something warm lapping at my boat, ushering me toward the shore, toward trusting that I am exactly where I should be. It is only through writing that I ever arrive anywhere. There is love on this shore. Love is where I am.

In the car, I look at myself in the rearview mirror. I love how I look. My eyes are calm, knowing that nothing can hurt me here. I neither seek to find nor fear to lose language at this moment. I have become language—spoken, pronounced, spelled out. I look at myself in the mirror. I am thirty-three years old, perhaps subconsciously willing my own resurrection, and no one else but my husband knows this: In our six years of marriage, we have never had sex.

PART ONE

HOW TO LOVE

1

FOR A LONG TIME, I can't understand why my grandmother Meropi hides her Bible under her pillow when the doorbell rings. Later, I learn what it means to live a secret Christian life in an atheist country like Albania: You have two lives—at least two—and you better keep track of which one stays at home and which one is allowed outside. My grandmother is a devout Christian who converted from Greek Orthodox to Seventh-day Adventist before the Second World War broke out. In 1990, when Communism collapses in Albania, she will be one of few Seventh-day Adventist survivors. For almost fifty years, she'll keep her tithe—$533.89—in a cookie tin until she is finally baptized in April 1992, at the age of eighty-seven, and can deliver her contribution to new missionaries from England.

When I am a girl, my grandmother is my world. After my parents pull me out of daycare, my grandmother moves in with us to raise my younger brother and me while they are at work. She follows me around the house with a glass of milk, some-times all the way out to the yard, so I can drink that daily dose, which I hate. She is a mouth of stories and prayers. She prays kneeling near a sofa, making sure it is the one facing north, and at night she prays like Daniel in the Bible. Sometimes I wake to her whole body in the moonlight, first standing in the room and then kneeling, then on her hands and feet, until she lies face down and whispers on and on for a good ten minutes.

"Nëna," I call, so she knows I am awake.

"Shhh, go back to sleep," she says. Other times, she laughs and says, "You're still awake, Ani? Come child, I'll pray with you," then approaches my bedside, kneels next to me, and begins: *O At, o Perëndi, kryetar i qiellit dhe i dheut* (Oh Father, oh God, ruler of the heavens and earth)—and I know God is all over, all around us.

I can still hear her telling me the story of Daniel in the lions' den and of Samson. My favorite part is when Samson finds honey in the belly of the slain lion. When my grandmother reaches this part, her lips soften and her speech slows down. I think she knows exactly where that honey came from, as though she's tasted it sometime in her past. Her lips and speech, even her gaze, have that knowledge.

On summer days, when my parents are at work, my grandmother lets me get lost on the floor with brown leather-bound Russian encyclopedias of literature. They are larger than my lap, so I have to sit on the floor with them. I don't know the language, but I can see the images in black and white, which leaves me spellbound. My mom jokes that Grandma knows exactly how to keep me entertained so she can read her Bible for hours. Anyone who knows her believes it. She lets me go out to the balcony, stand on a chair, and recite all the poems and nursery rhymes I know by heart to the neighborhood below. One day she counts. "She recited forty-one poems," she tells my parents. She will brag about it for years.

On winter mornings, when I get up early and she is still in bed, warm under the covers in a house that often has no heat, as is common in those days, she will say, "Give me your hands," and she will tuck them under her three or four blankets, inside her shirt, so they will warm up quickly against her soft flesh. And when I start school, she will kiss me each

That year winter threatened our small house.
I heard winds howl, but I had drawn enough stars
to burn in the stove to keep us warm.

morning before I go and read me a verse from the Bible. I can't leave the house until she reads the verse to me. It is the same for my parents and my brother. This is her way of sending us out into the world with the word of God on our shoulders, a protective hand, and I grow superstitious that getting good grades in school has everything to do with my grandma's ritualistic morning blessing.

In the spring and summer I capture living things—first butterflies, then fireflies, then snails and ladybugs, and ants and flies, then I simply pluck daisies and make chains to wear or put on my mother's head.

My best friend, a boy named Miri, runs with me for what feels like hours after lunch along the riverbank trying to capture monarch butterflies, yellow and orange, past the veiny violet flowers that old grandmas in the neighborhood say make really good tea. All I see is greenvioletyelloworange and Miri's white legs in his brown sandals running ahead of me, both of us wielding butterfly nets as he yells, "Come on Ani, run faster, get this one!"

On my birthday, my uncle Ladi gives me a see-through jewelry box. I fill it with blades of grass, a flower, a fly, an ant, a ladybug. Here, in the palm of my hand, I hold a whole forest. I watch to see how its inhabitants get along with each other. I add a dead ant to see if the others care, but soon discover there are no good Samaritans in nature.

When school starts, I long for long, sunny, summer holidays. When summer arrives, I spend it running, curious about the things that suddenly surround me. My brother and I chase lizards. We sit for hours waiting for them to come out of their holes. We throw stones at them. I always miss. We love to watch snails come out of their shells and sit quietly, expecting to see their delicate little horns emerge from their houses. They are such slow creatures, always coming into the outside world as if they are just being born. They make me impatient. I take a stone and hit one of them, but I don't kill anything.

Sometimes, when I am alone, I pick up shards of green bottle glass and look at the world through their width—a whole world, greens and greening. I can't take my eyes off it.

I have no stuffed toys, dolls, or much of anything to play with. The sidewalk is my toy, endlessly transforming, and green is everywhere: in the trees around our house, by the Lana River that runs close by, in the shards of broken wine bottles from the nearby Hotel Arbana, where many weddings take place on Sunday nights. Men and women drink till early morning, singing ballads that come at me from around all the corners of darkness over my bed. In the darkness, green is not seen. But did you ever squeeze your eyes shut, press on your eyelids till you'd see fireworks? A supernova of color.

I am trying to capture something that does not belong to me. But the child cannot relate to this. She is doing what comes naturally—chasing after living things, herself a brand-new living thing among them. When she makes daisy chains and gives one to her mother to wear, she is also pulling her mother into the world where they all belong. The petals are white and velvety. The sunlight pools around her ankles and over the entire field and time slows down. There is always enough time to make one more flower necklace, no matter how intricate the process. Or maybe this mother waits—and would wait forever—for the child to keep trying.

The butterflies, the ladybugs, the flies, the ants, all the living things captured, sometimes released, sometimes accidentally hurt or killed. She will spot them and point a finger like a child naming stars for the first time, a god standing next to her. But who is God now? And when does a child stop naming the world to herself?

2

I meet my husband Ishan through an online poetry workshop when I am twenty-two years old. He is twenty. We come to know each other online, too. I am a young immigrant in the U.S., and he lives in India. The members of the workshop come from all over the world. I have been in the States for four years, and have just begun to feel comfortable writing in English; it is a time when I can't stop writing poetry.

Ishan and I connect instantly while critiquing and exchanging our work, through our love for literature and words. He loves how I write about places and people. I love his acrobatic sentences. His poetry is strange, describing a life so remote and distant from the one I have lived in Albania and in the U.S. He writes beautiful, memorable narratives with extended similes and original, vivid metaphors about lives dominated by strong male figures, barbers, village people, and cows that "huddled like piles of laundry in the middle of the street." He weaves images effortlessly out of the air. People talk of love at first sight. For us, from the start, it is love at first words.

The first time Ishan sends me something in the mail, it is an odd-looking package—a thick envelope wrapped in gauzy material that smells of closets in locked rooms no one lives in, rooms I somehow already know I have been in. It smells like soil, this idea that someone all the way in India has something to say to me. I am alone at home when it arrives, take it upstairs to my room, sit on the floor, and open it: Ernest Hemingway's *For Whom the Bell Tolls*, a book he loves, with two large notebook pages written back-to-back in his sparse, hurried handwriting, but with which you can tell he has taken greater care. Inside Hemingway's book, I find pressed leaves from the trees around Ishan's town and a few photos. He has sent them because he knows I like pressing flowers and leaves in my own books.

He has also sent photographs. The first one shows him and his best friend, Ashok, outside Ishan's father's U-bolt manufacturing factory. Two young teenagers in flip-flops, T-shirts, and jogging pants sit against the wall. Ashok looks at the camera, smiling, whereas Ishan looks straight ahead to his left with that big smile on his face I will later recognize as his look after he has cracked a joke. They are sitting at the foot of the wall, a window with iron bars above them. The wall around the window is painted sloppily in limewash, the foundations of the building coming undone where it meets the ground. Rocks and red dirt at their feet. The end of the wall and the beginning of the earth don't quite fit each other, like fillings or crowns in your mouth that no longer sit well within your gums. Ishan fits perfectly in this landscape, and at the same time, he doesn't. If a person were in the dictionary under the word *liminal*, that would be Ishan. Even in photographs, maybe because he's got style, maybe because his body is constantly on the move, he's the type of person who never looks the same twice. He is here and he isn't and it is always like that.

In his letter, he says I am his home and asks me to make him my home. Soon, he writes, we will be home together. He believes it, so I believe it. It is like this pulsing beacon, seemingly so tangible yet just out of reach. When you first begin to believe in love, you are invincible in your eagerness, green.

I know I will meet Ishan long before we meet. It is happening. I am moving east. These days I hold on to this idea of a powerful thing two people can create that transcends all boundaries, geographical, cultural, religious, racial. It makes perfect sense that love will conquer all. That two people can manifest a whole future out of a house of words. Because words speak the truth, right?

Though I find his long emails stifling from repetitive professions of love and sense the naivete in both of us, I find myself writing long, repetitive, stifling emails in return. It seems to be coming out of this well of love, one that convinces you that your bond is real and one of a kind. Is it an obsession? Call it by its right name. *Need*. It is the best kind of dream a young poet weaves.

The attention we give each other through words, via email, for two years before we meet has a blooming effect: We energize each other. When my mother grows a new plant, she tells me the more she goes near it or talks to it and strokes its leaves very gently, the crazier it blooms. "She turns all her flowers toward me," she says of her petunias, and I picture them exploding like a flare on her balcony.

Ishan and I write each other pages and pages each week. If you're a writer, and you don't censor your thoughts when speaking to someone, and that person writes you back without censoring themselves in return, you enter this vortex of loving-the-self-in-love. It happens very slowly at first, while you're inching toward it one email at a time, and then like a spider sucked into the shower drain, you fall in, very deep, very fast, good luck getting back out! It's as though I am Narcissus who can't stop looking at his own image in the water—I can't stop writing, reading back what I wrote, and loving what I said. Can't stop reading and rereading what he said to me. At night, in dreams, I dream only words. During the day, I write to him, try to go to classes, and write poems. I am writing all the time. There is this sense of being drenched by language. Neither of us wants to put a stop to it.

For a while, I live my life inside my head: composing emails, reading them, writing poems, posting them, critiquing other people's work, and reading their critiques of mine in online poetry workshops. As I'd done in my younger years in Albania, I've found a way to avoid interaction with real people, meeting someone new, making some friends. I have no such courage. I've lived in Boston for a year and a half and hardly know my way around the city.

I don't know how I manage to complete an advanced degree in English. I wanted to read and learn more and I had hoped, too, that a master's degree would help me find a teaching job faster. So I do it all. I am learning so much about craft and how I want to write. Some of the people I engage with only online become my first, real creative writing teachers: Laurel K. Dodge, James Lineberger, Scott Odom, Teresa Ballard, Lynzee, Jack Anders, Jenni Russell, and of course, Ishan. Living away from home and having the privacy of my own dorm room has only made things easier. That is, more possible to fully participate in a virtual life, rather than living one.

"You are the best part about me," he writes. "I love you."

"Stop telling me that you love me," I write back. "It can't be true since we haven't even met in person."

And then I don't hear from Ishan for days.

"Ani, I overdosed," he finally writes almost a week later. He has taken amphetamines and cough syrup, something he's told me he uses habitually like he does weed and alcohol, to write, or to simply forget he's not where he wants to be. But this time he nearly dies. He says he was afraid he had lost me for good, and he took too much. "The maid saved me, and a village homeopathic doctor."

I am shaken. Ishan has nearly died and I see myself, having tried to take my own life once when I was seventeen. On the edges of my thinking, I feel somewhat responsible. Without me, Ishan seems entirely alone. With me, he is alive, in charge, ready to go anywhere. We bring out the best in each other, and isn't that a good sign to look for? Soon after this episode I ask him to stop relying on weed and pills, and he does. Now there is an *us* to hold on to, which feels important.

When something bothers Ishan, time seems to slow down. It feels like I have to wait an eternity to find out what has happened to him and why. But overnight, after we talk about it, the clouds clear, as though the world has only known sunlight. Sometimes we write

The neighbors are fast asleep.
A boat
has been anchored
at the edge of the mind.

It won't set sail. Not tonight.
Not while you're away.

20

new poems and that is enough to put us in a better mood. He is happiest when he writes, but he has no local poetry community or resources. He loves his parents yet feels estranged from them, having been enrolled in a boarding school a thousand miles away at the age of six. He wishes he could move to America, a culture whose movies, poetry, and music he adores, and I begin to dream it might be possible.

After I finish graduate school, I take a teaching job in Thailand so I can be closer to India and finally meet Ishan. He will come to visit me in Thailand first, but before that, he sends me photos.

There in my hands are the people from his village and his father's factory workers.

In one of the photos, men tie up a cow with rope, preparing her for an operation, he says.

Fields of cows and goats and langurs.

Eggplant flowers.

Butterflies.

A temple with a rainbow above it.

Lush green rice fields and women workers in blue saris, red, yellow, orange, fuchsia, green, standing, walking in a line, tying a headscarf, watching their step.

Close-up of a dead lizard.

Children bathing naked in a muddy river playing their own made-up games.

Ishan in a field, smoking inside the rusty skeleton of a white sedan, the absent tires of which have made room for beautiful weeds to grow.

Clouds over green hills, a bird on a wire. Behind it in his handwriting: "On the way to work. All these places already know tum :-)."

Tum. The Hindi pronoun for *you.* We have learned several commonly used words from each other's languages—equivalents in Hindi and Albanian for *I, you, mine, yours, love, eyes, forever, stars, heart, happy, lips, neck, I love you, lots, fart, ass, cunt, asshole, jaan*—which has no equivalent in English but a similar one in Albanian—*xhan/shpirt* (soul/sweetheart).

We pepper our emails with these terms and when they reach me, in my mother tongue, from an Indian who speaks to me in English, he feels so familiar to me. I believe the same is true for him when I write with the few Hindi words I've learned. *Kisses on tumhare aankhen*, I sign off. Ishan is like my extended consciousness for a while—I talk to him in my head, I talk to him through all the emails and messages we write to each other. For about three years, he is out there in a remote village in India, so far away from Massachusetts. If I close my eyes in bed at night and imagine him, he is part of the universe I cannot grasp, yet am a part of. Whatever this is we're creating, we don't want it to end. One day, he calls me from India, and when I pick up I smell wet spring earth. I see this glow of a yellow afternoon, the kind of light that envelops the earth once the afternoon rain and clouds

We say good morning
even though you speak back to me
from another country
your voice barely reaching
like dry leaves falling off tall trees
over telephone wires
and rooftops, over this wind
that seems bound to keep them
endlessly suspended.

have cleared away. And I see him in my mind's eye inside a phone booth, calling me. He says it is raining outside. That it is yellow and it is the afternoon now.

In one of his handwritten letters he writes: "Sometimes I have a sadness I cannot reject. But I know you have it, too. And anyway, you make all my sadness all right."

It feels good, like discovering a kind of power. He often talks about not feeling at home with his own family. Being treated like a child by everyone.

The pictures he has sent me are like an inventory of his life in his parents' town, in his home, at his job at his father's factory and gas stations.

Pictures of his parents' bathroom, a geyser, incomplete plumbing on the wall.

Their sitting room, two large beds in it facing each other, two single portraits of the boys, as children, hanging on the wall above.

Corridors that lead to other rooms.

His brother's bathroom where he develops film.

Their gardens, magenta and pink bougainvillea along the white wall surrounding their house. Coconut trees.

A front yard lined with plants in terracotta pots.

The main gate and the side gate.

His driver, his gardener, his cooks, some servants.

Photos of ponds and rivers and banyan trees nearby. A small pond and clouds over mountains on Ishan's way to work where he sometimes stops "to talk to you" before we meet in person.

A portrait of his business manager and one of his accountants. Ishan is the marketing communications specialist.

A huge spider on a bathroom door.

A "paari" street shop that sells cigarettes and gasoline in plastic soda bottles just opposite one of the family-owned gas stations.

A cow in a field, two flies on its forehead, ears stretched out sideways like wings to take off and fly with.

Rain.

Another rainbow.

The dog kennels, two German shepherds inside—Zulu and Gomez, the hyper one.

How could you not love someone who has taken photos of the whole world around him to show you? The good, the bad, the beauty, the ugliness, death, life, lush greenery, rotting walls, and carcasses. Why would you not love someone who would give all this in one day? The date on each photo is the same.

When I grow up in the capital city of Tiranë, nearly everyone seems to own a black umbrella. The lights from the street lamps reflect off the black umbrellas in the rain, the black tree bark soaked wet, and the black asphalt, illuminating the way and making that darkness less ominous, more magical. The rain is soft, drizzly; it covers everything. Even during the day, even through overcast skies, light seeps through those sidewalks and asphalts.

There are no skyscrapers in Tiranë when I live there. I realize now that the memory of my city is so bright at times because the 1980s Tiranë sky is open and wide. The tallest buildings are uniformly five stories high, with the exception of three nine-story buildings near the center of the city and the fifteen-story International Hotel. When it rains, the city square looks like our house on days when my mom washes the floors and puts all the chairs above the table—no one can walk in until the floors have dried.

When the rain is heavy, no one goes out walking. We say, *Bie shi me gjyma* (It's pouring cauldrons) or *shiu si litarë* (rain like lengths of rope). Rains are frequent, especially in the spring and fall. When it rains, whatever is happening around us seems temporary. It is as if the rain makes everything better, at least for a little while.

3

I land in Bangkok one night in August. I feel the humidity as soon as I step out of the airplane onto the tarmac, like stepping inside a giant mouth. It is drizzling. The international university where I'll be teaching is two hours north. The airport van drives past villages, past giant, silent Buddha statues, Indian ones and Thai ones, past gas stations, driving on the left side of the road.

We arrive in Muak Lek around two in the morning. There are no lights. Trees from both sides of the road hold hands and necks and noses. Driving under them in the dark feels like passing through nature's womb. Only it doesn't feel like nature. Something stranger—a sense of eyelessness, and me pressing deeper and deeper into the unknown.

The first day at university, I am busy meeting everyone and forgetting their names. A family invites me for dinner at their house. I think of Ishan and how much more likely it is that we'll meet. I come back and pass out at 8:00 p.m., then wake up at two in the morning. I can't go back to sleep. Through the open window, in the distance, come the sounds of the early morning train. It feels like Thailand's first poem to me. It moves with the same slow rhythm as trains in Albania. I feel completely alone yet surrounded by my past. I cry the longest I've cried in years.

The next day and for weeks afterward, time passes quickly. In Bangkok, I walk past canals and the Chao Phraya River. Taking a boat is even faster than going by car. I go shopping with my new friends at the big markets, Chatuchak and MBK Center, which stands for Mahboonkrong, which foreigners can't pronounce.

I love listening to the Thai language. It is like hearing someone walk in wooden clogs down cobblestone streets. *Tao rai na kah* (what time is it?). *Talat* (market). *Pad pak boong fai daeng*—my favorite dish, so simple to make: Fry chilies and garlic in soy sauce, sauté morning glory, then add oyster sauce till the vegetable greens and the stems become succulent. Pour over steamed rice with more chili sauce on top. Pak Khlong Talat (flower market), where one of the sellers gives me a flower just because. This unexpected generosity is common among the Thai people I meet. It is easy to approach strangers even though I don't speak the language, or vice versa. They are always willing to help me and that, too, has something to do with the color of my skin. I've never encountered a benevolent gaze like theirs in other countries, one that is non-judgmental, although they love good gossip.

I also notice there is a limit to the kind of help Thai people give you. They will lead you within sight of water, but you have to figure out the rest. Imagine constantly being harassed by tourists with endless questions. I take this to be their way of teaching foreigners about their land and culture without making them lazy. I think this is why so many people love visiting Thailand. The Thai people don't just hand you the keys. They push you to check out the grounds yourself.

What I love most in Thailand is the rain. It comes daily, usually in the afternoon. After the rain, all kinds of little creatures come out. Mostly slugs and snails and winged ants that fly everywhere in what seems like armies of millions, but the next morning all you see on sidewalks are their wings, detached, evidence of strange battles. I see centipedes and millipedes, and a close relative of the scorpion, but not the real thing. I live with geckos and spiders and ants. Butterflies come out in fives or sevens around every bush and tree and over the grass; they chase each other for seconds and then take off in opposite directions. Sometimes it rains all night, and I will never forget waking to the sound of raindrops stepping out of the mouths of orchids, papaya and mango leaves, falling onto the grass, returning to earth, with a calculated laziness. Drops like footsteps. I imagine one of the college gardeners approaching my window wanting to see me. How old am I at this moment? Twenty-five.

The moon is a lantern
    in a neighbor's yard.
In that yard,
I sit across the moon,
    my silhouette on fire
wishing he could
    see me now.

The apartment I rent in Bangkok has a porch. Just outside it, the backyard stretches out into a grove that stretches farther into a large field bordering woods of eucalyptus and other trees. Someone brings cows to graze at the edge every afternoon and after I am done teaching, I come home and sit on the porch with a cup of coffee to watch this procession. The cattle are mostly white with horns, their ears pointing down. They trail west, about twenty-five of them, moving through slowly like winter rivers drowsy with their running. The chain ends with little calves in the back, one suckling on its mother's tit. A small dog skips behind them; another one, older, runs alongside the owner. I do laundry, then hang the clothes out in the backyard to dry. The cows moo. Koyals sing. Yellow and lime and black butterflies stitch their own messages in the air. Cowbells punctuate time like irregular commas and semicolons in a long essay without a single indented paragraph. The sun scorches but never mind that. Dragonflies dash back and forth over my head. And I envy those cows. They pass through the woods so ignorant and carefree, knowing the pace, trusting the path.

Out in the streets and markets of the town, dogs are everywhere. People keep them around because, according to Buddhism, ancestors may have reincarnated into those dogs. They kind of look as if they are singing, *Don't worry about a thing / 'Cause every little thing gonna be alright*. Yes, they Bob-Marley to me. Some of them seem to be trained to bark only at *farangs*, what Thai people call foreigners. But most of the dogs I see never bark. I love watching them wander. They are so light on their paws and mindless-looking, but there is something about them that makes me think of artists—they walk around recording everything they see without being noticed. There is an aura of indifference about them; they couldn't care less if you fell and drowned in the canal.

But maybe the most curious thing about Thailand is this feeling I get in small towns and villages that the whole place sparks with worship. The hairdresser I go to has a prayer branch, as he calls it, wrapped in golden foil, framed on his wall. "It's for good luck," he says. Other people's luck here takes root on top of a hill or by the side of a lake in the form of a Buddha statue or spirit trees wrapped in colored ribbons and marigold wreaths. In temples, people come to light candles in front of statues. I meet a woman there who tells me: "The god's eye is awake, look at it moving from left to right, see?" I want to tell her that it is only the flickering flame reflected on the statue's painted eye, but I don't. If she believes a statue can be awakened through praise and worship, it's not for me to make her understand otherwise.

Against this backdrop, half magical, half strange, sometimes frighteningly so, the time comes for me to meet Ishan in person. He is coming to visit me in Bangkok. I have waited for this day for so long. We both have. I tell my parents about it over the phone.

"You can't do this to us!" my mother yells in my ear from a world away. "Where are your brains? You're going to marry an Indian? And live in India? We came all the way to America so you could move to India?"

"Mom," I say, "you're going to make my heart stop. All I want is to meet this guy. I'm not marrying anybody! And I'm coming back!"

Despite how dramatic and loud these phone conversations get, I book two rooms at a bed and breakfast in Bangkok and take the van to the airport.

4

1881. Eighty kilometers from Albania's cultural capital of Korçë lies Trebickë: a small village of one-story stone houses and walnut, quince, cherry, and pear trees. Around Trebickë are the sister villages of Grabockë, Panarit, Treskë. Trebickë is made of two sections, Lower Trebickë near the Osum River, where it never snows, with its clamorous bazaar where people sell, buy, and butcher livestock, and Upper Trebickë, about a thirty-minute walk uphill where snow is guaranteed every winter.

Now see Nërënxa, a young woman of sixteen or seventeen years of age. She has just left the bazaar where she was buying groceries and begins the climb home, her hair a braid horseshoeing around her neck, though you can't see it under her white scarf. She's returning home to her widowed mother, Katerina, whose brothers have migrated to Aswan, Egypt. Nërënxa is an only child. It is late afternoon, the middle of winter.

Albania at this time remains occupied by the Ottoman Empire until it declares independence in 1912. But in 1881, Turkish soldiers walk in every city and village in the land. Here, too, two Turkish soldiers have been patrolling the bazaar, collecting taxes, when they notice Nërënxa. They are following her home, and one of them picks up his pace, telling her to wait, perhaps, he just wants to have a word, when she notices them and knows she has to run. There's no time to speak or scream. No one can help her here against the armed Turks.

Nërënxa runs and the Turks run faster. They pass St. Mary's Monastery, an equal distance between Upper and Lower Trebickë, and Nërënxa calls on Mary. She's Daphne calling out to Peneus, in another time, in another country. It's the same story, except Apollo is human here and getting closer.

"Mother, save me! The Turks!" Nërënxa screams when she's within a hundred feet of her own house. "They're after me!" she cries, and in those words, the cry of every woman and girl from every country, from now to antiquity.

She reaches the house and crosses the threshold, shutting the wooden gate behind her, but one of the men sticks his head through the small square window in the center calling, "Come out, come out, I won't hurt you!"

Her mother, Katerina, a tall woman dressed in black—as she will for the rest of her life to mourn her husband—has been standing, shoulders to the wall, behind the door. She lifts an ax overhead and in one swift motion chops off the soldier's head. See his head roll onto the stones in the front yard. His body suffers something like a tremor, lingers upright for a few moments, then collapses outside the door. The other Turkish soldier sees his friend's headless body drop and doesn't wait another second before running downhill as fast as he can.

Katerina and Nërënxa have no time to hug or say a word to each other. They pack their clothes in two large bags, mount them on their horse and leave Trebickë that night. They walk eighty kilometers and reach Korçë by morning. No one looks for them. In the village, everyone is proud of what a mother did to protect her daughter. They settle in Korçë.

Years later, Katerina passes away. Nërënxa marries and has two daughters. The youngest daughter will move to America with Nërënxa a decade after the turn of the century. The oldest one will stay in Korçë, where, in 1905, she gives birth to my grandmother, Meropi.

I come from a line of Daphnes. Our mothers would not think twice to give their lives to protect ours.

5

The day I meet Ishan, it is my twenty-sixth birthday. He has just turned twenty-four. We have been corresponding for three years—now we are meeting for the first time in a country foreign to both of us.

He looks so young when I see him, and beautiful. A huge smile on his face, eyes so brown; thick, straight, tar-black hair that falls over one side of his face.

Like me, he is shy, creative, pensive, sad, and nervous. I feel an instant affinity with him. To this day, I can close my eyes and still see his caterpillar-green shirt. In fact, as he walked toward the waiting area, all I could see was a flash of green and his smile. For me, he was that Rumi poem: *Out beyond ideas / of wrongdoing and rightdoing, / there is a field.* He came to meet me there. So did I. All the way to Thailand. Maybe *I* was the Rumi poem.

He says: *Hey, Anu.*

I don't remember what else we say or if I say anything back, but next thing I know we're in a taxi and I'm holding my mouth with both hands because I feel carsick. I throw up in my mouth because there is nowhere else to throw up and we laugh about this years later. "That's how you really felt," he will say.

He can't keep his eyes off of me. His eyes and his camera those days, even when I'm putting on makeup in the morning or walking ahead of him. It annoys me and I tell him so, but I also understand it's his way of having proof: what has been dream-like for so long is finally real.

I've booked two separate rooms in a small bed and breakfast on Soi KasemSan 1 but we spend the whole first day in his room. From the beginning, it is evident I won't be keeping mine.

Those first few hours together he shows me albums and albums of his family, his childhood, his young mother and father in 1970s and '80s India. They are beautiful—his tall father with blue bell-bottom pants and longish, thick, straight hair from a Beatles album and his slender, youthful mother with a slightly concerned look on her face. In one of the photos, she sits on the floor, legs in a V, little toddler Ishan lying flat on his back between them as she's holding his arms down with her legs and feeding him rice with a spoon. In another, she's hugging him from behind and holding his chin toward her as if to say to something unknown and unseen: *He's mine, you'll never have him.*

33

Pictures of Ishan in boarding school in India. He has gone through at least two of them, Welham Boys School and St. Paul's. His parents first send him there when he is six years old. He is eighteen when he gets out. We look at photos of him in uniform, him and his friends, Ishan pissing near a cliff, all the boys huddled together, mountains, Ishan in costumes in drama class. I love all the lives he has lived already and he is only twenty-four.

He is a little uneasy talking about the boys in these schools. I sense he will never tell me exactly what happened in those years and yet I also sense I already know. We have had similar paths dealing with harassment and sexual abuse, though I won't find this out till years after our divorce. I ask him about it and he becomes uneasy; he shrinks and twists up his face like having tasted something sour and lets out a sigh that is half sigh, half curse in Hindi: "Tcheeeeh," he says, "they made me do stuff . . . ," and then, "I don't want to talk about it," in a very dry, firm tone like an ax chopping off the conversation's head. I don't remember asking him again. But I know that, like me, he has dealt with the anxiety and shame that comes from prolonged abuse. Now that I think about it, maybe he is like me in this way—he doesn't know how to talk about it because that whole period of his life has seeped like a virus into his language, distorting it and his capacity to name his own experiences. Language isn't lost, exactly. But it isn't time to speak of it yet.

We have been sitting looking at photos for a while when he takes out a box from his pocket and a gold ring with seven tiny diamonds appears on my finger.

"What are you doing?" I ask. I am shocked and somewhat uncomfortable.

"It's your birthday!" he says, beaming. "I wanted to get you something on your birthday!"

It looks like an engagement ring. "How am I going to wear this at work?" I say. "It only fits on my ring finger. They'll think I got engaged."

Why don't I say more? Because when Ishan gets hurt, whether in person or by email, I feel hurt, and he shuts down. I also like the ring he's chosen. Atypical. The tiny diamonds arranged like a flower.

Later he shows me two silky, black woven bracelets someone in his village made. They're like prayer bracelets. He will wear one and I will wear one.

"We can put them on right now and I'll burn the endings. You can take it off when the threads tear on their own."

It fascinates me, the idea of wearing something on my body day in and day out, through showers, through sleep, while teaching, always there. He will have one, too. It feels both like a commitment and like something young people do. So I do it. Because that's what I am: young. Have hardly even dated anyone. It is the same for him. This is how we bind each other. First, he helps me put mine on. Then he burns the ends with his lighter and the knot burns shut forever. Then I help him. We have woven bracelets tied around our left wrists. They are black. I love black, but the fact that this black is tied to me with such permanence makes me feel uneasy. I feel marked, almost cursed. I brush the feeling off. I don't believe in those things, I tell myself.

We haven't kissed yet, but later he tells me I made the first move and was all over him. Fine. Maybe I was.

We walk to MBK Center next door to get a drink and sit facing each other. Ishan gets a glass of Coke and I sip coffee. We look like two teenagers, giddy and high. I don't notice anything else around me, except him.

"You're so beautiful."

Who said that? I think that's what he kept telling me.

"I love you, Anu."

I say it back. I don't even check myself. I say it back.

That first night together we can't wait to get our hands on each other and start undressing, but when Ishan wants to go a little further I stop him.

"I haven't done that before." I can't even name it.

"I haven't either," he says.

"Yes, but I won't do that. Not before marriage."

"What?" he asks, half laughing, half in shock.

"I can't. I really believe I should wait for that."

"You're so funny," he says. "What's the difference between going all the way and having shown me your boobs or lying here half-naked?"

He has a point, I think. And soon I will discover he can debate anybody on any topic and will always get the last word. I have no answer. But I am determined not to have sex this time. I grew up in a home where all the adults hardly ever spoke about sex, and when they did, it was in the context of waiting to have sex after marriage according to teachings in the Bible.

But I wanted to wait because I didn't know anything about how to have sex with someone. I believed I knew everything I needed to know about love—an unshakable strong feeling toward someone you want to share and create a new life with. I felt this love toward Ishan, but all the voices from my religious upbringing were louder than my earlier self-discovered beliefs about the body, the ones that had already taught me, in childhood, how to touch myself, how to want to be touched, how God wanted me to know my own body.

That night we sleep side by side. At first, his body twitches when he lies down on the bed, hiding and showing and hiding his face on the pillow. He reminds me of a timid child hiding his face in his mother's lap when he's told he's beautiful.

I want to kiss you.

Maybe I say it, or he does, but when I look at him, his lips only part. No words come out.

Our bodies grow, willing toward each other the way vines will themselves to walls. Then sometime later, the weight of his sleep falls on my arm and ribs when he dreams. Relaxed muscles and bones. I feel as if I can enter his flesh and sleep there, tucked in, dreaming he will never wake.

I enjoy watching his body, like when it opens conversations in the morning downstairs by an orchid flower, two cups of coffee, toast, butter and jam, the B&B owner smiling at us. When Ishan talks, it is like someone has flung open doors to a ballroom where the whole town has come to celebrate his return. He is all hands and throwing his head back in laughter.

I love the dimple on the left corner of his mouth, the hard stars on his chest. His hands reach and find mine when we're in a crowd where he knows I'm nervous, and now, in the privacy of this room, it's enough to lightly touch his knuckles, nest my own into his palms, or interlace our fingers and feel like our bodies are made to birth stars. That night, I feel as though I have entered his body, never to come out. He is like that, to be added to—like salt to flour—never to part from. The hammock of his neck.

One night Ishan wakes up startled, screaming, and slaps me.

"It's me. It's me, Ishan. It's Ani. It's Ani," I repeat, my heart in my mouth.

"I'm so sorry," he says, nearly crying. "I had a horrible dream. Horrible, horrible, Anu. Hold me." And he starts crying. He is shaking.

A moment later, he gets up and curls into a ball on the floor sobbing.

"I'm no good for you. I can't be with you. You should go. Go very far away, Anu."

"What are you talking about, Ishan? We will figure this out together, okay? Come back to bed. Please?"

I beg for a while. He lies on the floor, in the dark, a formless breathing thing like a story that has no ending or beginning. It will often be like that with Ishan—we will be the happiest one moment, and the next he will leave me for his mind, going over and over something I don't fully understand.

That first week, we spend a day in the historic ancient city of Ayutthaya. It is Songkran, the traditional Thai celebration of the New Year. We have booked a taxi for the day and the driver takes us around key tourist spots. We walk through ruins, taking lots of photos. Ishan keeps lagging behind, taking photos of my butt, photos of me looking toward him, looking at things. I feel stalked, but that's not all. We are poets. We have been in touch with each other for three years. And now we are in a place of ruins, in love, so young and immortal. We both believe it and we are somewhat fascinated with each other. In a place of such strong worship culture, we fit right in. We worship each other. He's on the whole time. Where does he get this energy? We never stop walking. And kissing. Except to eat. He sticks his hand in his backpack and pulls out a bottle of Hajmola candy.

"You have to try this, it smells like *pordhë*"—the Albanian word for *fart*—"but feel how sour it is. Don't you love it?" he asks, laughing hard, then popping one in his mouth. I try it. FIRE! He kisses me.

"Fucking fire, Ishan, what the hell is this!"

But he's right, it's one of those childhood-type candies, so disgusting you can't not love it.

On the way back to my school, we pass a crowd painting their faces white and wetting each other with water. We roll down the taxi windows and let them paint our cheeks and wet us. In the photo we take, we look exactly the same.

One morning during the weeks we stay at my school, I ask Ishan to take a van to Bangkok for the day so I can be alone. He gets very upset. "I would never ask you to go away from me, Anu," he says. "You're my home. How can you ask your home to be away from you? What is wrong with you? You're crazy."

I don't understand. I feel overwhelmed, but then I rationalize that this is just how he is. When he wants something, he wants it all. If that's who he is, I can't change it. But why am I feeling uncomfortable? How can I ask my home to be away from me? The more he asks, the more I begin to believe he has a point.

At school, everyone is curious about the ring on my finger. I am summoned to the HR office and told my housemate has expressed concern that when Ishan visits me in my room, we close the door. I should keep it open in the future if we are in the same room alone, she says. She lets me know this is not coming from her, but it has made my roommate uncomfortable. I understand. We live on a Seventh-day Adventist college campus.

Another friend calls me a dark horse when we are with a group of our single friends. This is the first time I've heard the phrase and I like it.

What I love most about Ishan is the fact that he loves me. All those love poems and long emails. Sometimes he kisses me on the forehead or holds me for a little longer. That is home. When I am upset, he has the right words to comfort me. He knows how to make me feel better and is always good at making me laugh. He knows how to be a good friend. He is easy to be myself with, easy to talk to. No guard. I have come from a culture of erasure: people erasing other people out of spite, for sport, for power. In his best moments, Ishan is someone who listens to my thoughts. God makes sense to us both, as much as prayer does when we pray together. He often asks me to pray for him, especially if he has to travel somewhere far or take an exam. He trusts in the faith I have in what I ask for.

This time of year, snow falls in my
  grandparents' little town.
You, like my grandfather, love chilies.
  I slice them into thin rings
and throw them in a round, white
  porcelain cup filled with
Kikkoman. We have basil chicken for
  supper and you let me have
your last bite, like a promise for me
  to outlive you.

I love the fact that he has learned some Albanian and often asks me what we call this or that in my language. He comes up with random acts of kindness. "Let's give this much to your parents," he might say, or "Let's give this to our landlord." We go to a market to buy jewelry and he says, "Buy this one, too," or "This would look great on you." He is excited when I am happy. When we stop at a street market and find handmade drawings framed in bamboo shoots, I want to buy two or three as souvenirs. We walk out with at least ten. He doesn't hold back when he knows something will make me happy.

6

When I think about Albania, I think about childhood. My childhood as a movie. I think about Communism. A collective performance. If I am to take you there, I have to feed you a kind of nationalistic stew every family consumed every day until a few years after Albania's Communist Leader, Enver Hoxha, died. Many still consume it to this day.

Don't get lost here. In order to tell the story of my childhood, I must distort the narrative—reality itself was distorted. That was the nature of language at the time. One piece of truth on the radio, another on the street, another behind closed doors, and you have to keep up with piecing it together just as the TV, newspapers, slogans on the walls of every school, library, museum, hospital, and government building dump their landfill of "news" on you daily. How do I make this real for you? I have to take you inside the chef's kitchen. Who cooks such a thing? How? Why can't people stop eating this stew?

It's an absurd story about a period ruled by absurdity, made real through a child. When adults recall this time, they resort to finger-pointing, sharp nails shoved straight into each other's chests, mouths so loud they want to swallow silence from one another's faces.

The child remembers long meetings on TV. So many people on the screen for long hours sitting and standing, raising a fist, clapping, Enver Hoxha talking. He has a sweet smile, like a lamb. Everyone knows he likes children best and the children sing of the sweetness of his hands and the luck of the Labor Party to be ruled by someone like him.

In the house, the adults often counsel, "Don't talk about God to your friends." *Besë ki, besë kujt mos i zë* (Have faith, but trust no one). Others come to visit, an aunt, an uncle and his family, friends of the parents. They sit and talk, drink coffee, read their fortunes in the patterns of their cups' coffee grounds, make *byrek* together. My grandmother reads the Bible only to

42

us and her other son when he comes to visit. Her cousin who lives in America visits in 1986 and buys us a color TV. An army of adults and children from our ten-family building comes to watch the World Cup on our living room floor. Italy loses long before the finals and I'm inconsolable. It takes a while before my mom finds me where I'm hiding, out on the balcony.

Enver Hoxha's speeches and plenums play daily on TV and radio, or are published weekly in the pages of *The People's Voice*, until everyone hears them as their own voice and chants right back. Whispers of people thrown in jail and "disappeared" spread in the streets and apartment halls when people come home from work, lingering in their doorways to talk to neighbors. Like a good stew that must cook slowly, where repetitive motion is key, broadcasts of lavish parades and movies made to praise the status quo are played across the country at regular intervals.

"They knew everything about you, they knew even the things you didn't know," my mother tells me. "I once met a Kosovar poet at a literary conference in 1973 in Korçë who bought my first book of poems. After the conference in Korçë, he traveled across Albania and sent me postcards from the different cities telling me what he was up to there, and that he was reading my book. I did not get the postcards, but I was called in to the office of the Corps Commissioner of Korçë instead.

"'What are your intentions for communicating with this Kosovar poet?' he asked me. 'Do you know that he writes about Tito?'"

Tito, otherwise known as Josip Broz Tito, was the president of what was then Yugoslavia from 1945 until his death in 1980.

Although Kosovars are and speak Albanian, the Communist regime in Albania was so isolationist that Communist Albanians held their own Albanian brothers and sisters of Yugoslavia at arm's length like they did everyone else abroad.

"'I never received the postcards,'" I told him. "'I have never read his books and don't know what's in them.'

"But the truth is he never wrote about Tito," my mother tells me. "They lied and put pressure on you so you would crack. Shortly after, they called me into the office again and told me to keep an eye out and report anything that looks suspicious in the behavior or words of other colleagues. I left that meeting wondering, what could I report about? There was nothing I wanted to do with this. I shut the door behind me and never set foot in that office again."

One year later, an officer who worked in Korçë is transferred to a higher position at the Ministry of the Interior in the capital city and finds my mother's book of poetry and the postcards sitting in a drawer in the office he now works at. He calls another poet he thinks might know my mother and asks her to return everything to her.

My mother never meets this man, but when I think of him, I think of those single flowers that somehow manage to break through concrete.

I know about status when I am very young. If your family members work for the government, that is a plus. If there is a *stain* in their biography, that is a minus.

"What's a stain, Mom?"

"It's when you've done something the Party doesn't like."
Subconsciously, I make a list:

1. My uncle is a movie producer/director—he has a picture on his bookshelf of himself shaking hands with Enver Hoxha. We all have a copy of this picture and display it on our bookshelves. (+)
2. My mother is a poet who writes mostly love poems and not much about the Labor Party. (−)
3. My parents are not members of the Communist party. (−)
4. My grandmother is a secret Christian; some neighbors have begun to suspect it. (−)
5. Lillian, my grandma's first cousin, lives in the U.S. (−)
6. All other uncles and aunts have the same one- or two-bedroom apartment furnished with the same couches, bookshelves, tables, kilims, fridge, phone, black and white TV. (+) (+) (+) (+)

Nobody I loved was taken into the woods and shot.

When certain neighbors begin to drop by your house very early or very late, there's a different rhythm to the day. Your radio is switched on to a local news channel, *The People's Voice* newspaper spread open on the table—to survive, you master the art of obscuring your own reality.

Children of entire generations are raised hearing "don't"—no one says, "You can do it." The dream to be different is short-lived because the fear of not fitting the mold of a collective is ingrained. You are pushed only when your performance is

Last night I saw my father in
   a dream running through a
   field.
He was a black figure. The field
   was two long red arms
stretched out around him. He
   was running from something.
There they were. They were keys.
   They were eyes, eyes like keys.
They were eyes. They were keys.
   From the nape of his neck,
they began to pry him open like a
   treasure box.

measured against that of everyone else's. You're never measured against yourself.

When the adults gather, they chant: "Don't show weakness. Don't bow down to anybody. Let them burst with jealousy." This is when you learn that saying sorry is a weakness and you're forty years old before you realize what it means to have compassion for yourself.

When Enver Hoxha dies on April 11, 1985, I am in the first grade. Our teacher enters the room and tells us to pack our bags because something has happened and we need to leave and they will tell us when we get there.

When we get where? What has happened?

We don't walk for long, though it seems like forever until we come to an open field and each class and its teacher sits in circles on the grass. And there they tell us.

"We've just heard this morning that Comrade Enver Hoxha has died."

Each of the teachers begin to weep. All my classmates, too. The whole field is weeping and crying and it confuses me a great deal. I can't cry. I feel nothing. Someone has died. I don't even understand what that means. The country's leader has died. That too, I can't connect to. I can't cry like everyone else and that is confusing and upsetting me even more.

"You can go home now," the teachers say, "and think about this." We scatter like bats out of a cave.

When I get home, I find my grandmother watching TV and crying, too.

Everyone feared Enver Hoxha. They feared him so much that in his death they were seized with fits of hysterics lest they be found unworthy followers. I didn't understand it then, and never asked, but now I wonder if my grandmother was relieved that the man who had turned the whole country atheist had finally lost his grip on what everyone chose to think about God.

Behind windows, black and white screens broadcast a long

Congress, but we didn't
    understand a word.
When we heard the truth, we took it

for another story grown-ups told
to put us to sleep.
    Behind our building,

the river grew tired,
    rocks rattled in the dark.
We awoke in spring, our bodies

overgrown with weeds. Our parents
had no idea how to save us.

I had just turned seven. I sat on the floor and wrote my first poem—a direct address to the month of April and how it had made everyone cry now that we had lost our president.

Prill o prill
na mbushe sytë me lot
se xhaxhin Enver
nuk e gjejmë dot.

For years after the collapse of the Communist regime, I imagine a collective of Albanian families sitting down at the table uniformly at the same time. See them now through the windows of their houses. They sit with the biggest smiles on their faces, the children, the father, the grandparents if there are any, and the woman of the house. She is the only one standing, ready to put food in their bowls.

47

She could be smiling, too, but you can't see it. Or if you do, you don't recognize it as a smile. It is the way her lips have been permanently sewn shut and everyone seems pleased that it is so. She, too, has convinced herself it's the mark of a great hostess.

Once the food is laid out in the bowls, people begin to eat. The texture is the best part. It settles in the bowl like a mass of loose scree and everyone chews on it with teeth they have taken great care to sharpen and prime for the occasion. It is rocks on rocks. There is gnashing. And their smiles grow bigger after each bite as their teeth loosen and fall. Each window is a bright eye, wide open, watching, making sure that the other windows in the neighborhood are also wide open and the people are doing the same thing. It is important to everyone behind each window to know that those behind the window next door are following along, and have enough of the same to consume. If anyone notices that a family is lacking, the man of the house will go over and bring stew to his neighbors. "My wife Leonora made this. Eat. Enjoy. May it be blood and fat to you. Long live the Labor Party!"

Of course this is not what really happened. But this is one way a child processes tyranny.

After Hoxha's death, the Albanian people don't understand what to do with freedom. It's as though no one knows how hungry they have been. A new morning dawns where yesterday's rulers find themselves in high offices again and those who had been suffering all along in internment camps are cast away, their voices, their names erased once again. When a tyrant dies, the cycle does not break unless there is acknowledgement, change, forgiveness. In my country, even thirty years after the collapse of Communism, there has been no acknowledgement of the toxic years so many died and suffered from. The venom of the past still runs in the Albanian government's veins.

Some things do change after the dictatorship crumbles. Many people leave the country and many others move into the cities from smaller villages on the periphery. Women and men who sat cross-legged on street or school corners selling sunflower seeds and the most delicious green plums are replaced first by other women and men sitting on stools selling chewing gum, cigarettes, pocket tissues on small wooden tables, and then replaced by tents or small aluminum and plastic kiosks built overnight, only to be replaced yet again by larger stores and mini-markets.

The only thing that remains constant is my grandmother's faith, her compassion for every human being she comes in contact with. She is faithful before and during Communism. She remains faithful after. So many believe in her prayers and will ask her to pray for them. In my mind, she is fluent in understanding that language has a soul, that how we use words can heal or curse. Whenever I think of what I love most about Albania, it is this: The most ordinary women whose lives and convictions remain unruled by the extraordinarily absurd times they live through. I name them to myself and they are always with me: Katerina, Nërënxa, Meropi, Garufo, and my mother, Julia.

IN INDIA THERE'S A NAME FOR YOU

7

WHEN I FINALLY VISIT ISHAN in India, it is for the Christmas holiday. It is the second time we've met in person.

I land in Calcutta after 10:00 p.m., after a short flight that feels like an eternity. The man sitting next to me harasses me so much I ask the stewardess to change my seat. I am relieved to be off the plane, though I feel very small in the crowd of people gurgling through exit doors to meet their families. Ishan is right there waiting for me just where he had explained he would be. I feel relieved that he does exactly what he says he will do. Outside, taxi drivers swarm to take us in, but his family driver has come to pick us up.

We drive through a lit highway, windows down. It is December, still warm but with a comforting coolness in the air. My own family is so far away. I feel completely compassless, unmoored, untethered.

If I resemble anything in the universe at this time, it is a tiny drop of mercury suspended in the deep dark, unable to attach to anything, yet ready to merge with the first other mass of mercury to pass by.

In Calcutta, we enter Ishan's grandparents' house and I meet his aunt and some of his cousins. That night we sleep in a bedroom where Ishan's parents stay when they visit. I am introduced to other people throughout the next day, feeling a little awkward because everyone wants to know, who is this girl? How did you meet? What does this mean? Where will you live? I read this minute detailed investigation across their faces. They keep looking at me but don't ask questions. Or maybe I'm projecting onto them what I think my Albanian relatives would have asked.

A few days later, we walk into Howrah Railway station to catch an overnight train to Kesinga, in Orissa, where Ishan's family lives. We arrive at the station in the evening, the whole place lit by a golden glow. The walls, the air, the people. So much movement, yet it all feels stationary. Maybe all stations feel that way by definition—they will always be there despite the daily motion through them. Beggars and hardworking laborers ask to carry our luggage, middle-class and lower-class men, women, and children standing, sitting, squatting, some sleeping on the floor. It is like walking through paintings within larger paintings, everyone waiting to pass through to their own destination. A little girl makes eye contact with me. I don't know what she sees in me or if she wants to tell me something. The way I am being looked at makes me feel indecipherable. I feel the same way about them. I have no idea what their lives are like. Feeling like I have puzzled these people is better, I think, than feeling like they want to pierce into me, a constant feeling I grew up with in Albania.

We board the train and one of the conductors looks at us a few seconds too long as he inspects our tickets to make sure we are supposed to be in the private sleeping compartment.

We hardly sleep. There's a photo I have from that night in which I'm in the background, blue hat on, feet under the covers and both my fists under my chin. Ishan is taking a selfie of us and I'm smiling and he is doing that thing again, sucking in his cheeks as if he needs to look thinner. But you can tell he likes how he looks in it and maybe he also likes that I'm right there next to him.

The next morning, his driver, Surrendra, has driven ahead to pick us up for the last three hours' drive of the journey. He has the exact smile I've seen in a photo; throughout the ride, he cannot stop smiling. He adores Ishan and would do whatever Ishan asks. One of those things you pick up in the exchange of laughter and banter between them. One of those things I have always loved about Ishan—how close he is with all the people that work for his family.

We stop at a dam on the way that Ishan wants to show me. It is peaceful. No one else is here. I move a stone or two, as if to remind myself I did pass through here.

A dam is a barrier by definition, and yet I don't remember what the dam looked like or if there was any water. All these years later, thinking of it, I see myself surrounded by signs telling me to turn back, that I do not fit in this picture. But I also see something else, something perhaps American in me. For the first time in my life I am making my own choices. Up until this point, I have lived the majority of my life in Albania, obedient to my parents in a predominantly patriarchal culture. Then I move to America and learn about women—people in general— exercising their own will, finding their own voice.

I see myself at the dam where I don't remember if there was any water and I know that girl is relying on herself. She has to find out where these choices will take her. She doesn't *see* or *listen* well enough, perhaps. But she is determined to make these choices for herself, free of parental, cultural, or religious community control. She feels empowered and I will always be proud of that girl.

We reach the house the next afternoon and Ishan's parents come out to greet us. Ishan's mother looks upset, curious, piercing. She does not smile. His father, too, looks serious, tall, grounded, maybe the only one who is present in the moment.

Ishan bends down and touches their feet. Then we go into Ishan's room where I see his bathroom. I recognize it from the photos and I start bawling. I cry so hard, I scare Ishan.

He asks again and again what is wrong. "I don't know. I don't know," is all I allow myself to say. I keep all language inside me. I cry like that for a good while and then fall asleep.

I cry so hard and I don't want to recognize the reason why. At first all I see is that Ishan's house is bare—there is little furniture, a carpet, and a large, dark portrait of a very stern, solemn-looking great-grandfather on the wall in the dining room. I have expected to fall in love with his home as I had fallen in love with him, but the two do not align. Instead, I feel an absence of his personality. This isn't his style. It doesn't occur to me at this moment that the house can't be in his style. He has hardly lived here. I also realize that my parents sacrificed everything for me and my brother to have a better future, more financially independent than theirs, but I cannot see what financial independence with Ishan is going to look like. I see into the future, already married to this man, already having abandoned and disappointed my parents. Maybe this was anxiety. Maybe it was evidence of the kind of guilt a child of immigrants constantly lives with.

I sleep in Ishan's room and he sleeps in his grandfather's. This is the arrangement. But every morning Ishan sneaks into my bedroom and we have the same dialogue:

"What are you doing? They're going to mind this."

"Will you quit worrying! It's fine. They know that we're going to wait."

"But what will they think?"

"Oh, shush. Come here!"

And we lie there for a few extra hours kissing and holding each other and laughing about what the maids and cooks are thinking until a maid or cook knocks on the door with food or asks us to go out so they can start cleaning.

Ishan has no friends in his hometown—all his friends from boarding schools live in other cities and provinces far away. But

I love how he interacts with his driver, cook, and other servants, asking after their families. Sometimes I think he's closer to them than to his own parents. To him, the driver and gardener are not just people who fulfill those roles, but individuals who've acquired a certain wisdom we're lucky to learn from.

I love the maids, Bhama in particular. Her laughter is like the sound of her anklet when she waters flowers in the garden. When she smiles, her eyebrow becomes a little lizard twitching before finally finding rest.

The first time Ishan's mom really lets herself laugh in my presence is when I tell Ishan we all should cook a Christmas meal for the maids and the cooks. He tells his parents.

"Listen to this, Ani says we should make a nice Christmas dinner for the maids and cooks."

Laughter breaks out. I am certain neighbors and monkeys down the street can hear it.

I want to give something in return to these people who work so well and so quietly for so little. But this is not done.

"They'd immediately take advantage of you, Ani," explains his mother. "You can't mix with them like that. They need to remember who's boss."

These days "Ya Ali" plays on the radio constantly, a song from an old Bollywood movie I've never watched. It is playing the day Ishan's driver takes us around Kolkata to buy bootlegged movies and jewelry. The phrase is a call to God, but I don't know what the rest of the song means except for the feeling I get discovering this person I have waited to be with, his family, his culture, the little village in Orissa he is from, where the sun lingers in the afternoons, and a film of canary gold silkens the horizon where cows graze, banyan trees holding roots with one another like young people in love who tangle themselves with so many promises.

"You know what I love, I love the stench of piss after the rain in Kolkata's railway station," he says as we are out walking in the city together. He says things I've never heard anyone else say; sometimes I think he does this for effect. I love the joy in him. He is the *Cowboy Junkie–Kurt Cobain–Eddie Vedder–Nick Drake–Peter Green–I'm gonna die by twenty-eight, you'll see–I'm the god of fuck–I'm beautiful* kind of loud, wild guy shielding perfectly the most vulnerable side within.

There isn't much to do in this village. We play cards, UNO, Ludo, and other board games together. Ishan and I, or Ishan and I and his parents. I can't go out and take a walk. It will disturb people's peace and way of life, I am told, because I will stand out.

One day we go on a picnic with the whole family. We drive to a remote field and set up under the shade of a large banyan tree. You can hear cicadas and koyals and the wind. The sound of the koyal, so new, suddenly taking dominion over the landscape in short-rising pitches, seems to both alarm and lull you into slumber. In the distance, villagers try to get a glimpse of who we are, why we are there. I see them smiling. Being naive, I say I would want to meet them, but Ishan's father jokes that they would kidnap me.

"But they can't do that," he adds. "You're the princess of Kesinga."

A little farther from us, on the other side of the field, cows, and on top of their backs, white egrets that alight and return like dreams. There are no houses as far as the eye can see. I don't know who owns this land, but right now, just standing, looking at it all, I feel that my heart owns it. Late afternoon sunlight and the amber-colored earth paint this whole memory in gold and honey. I could live here forever, I tell myself. Home is a place where there's calm within and without.

The day after Christmas, a 9.1 magnitude earthquake occurs in the Indian Ocean. We are far away and do not feel it. The earthquake triggers a tsunami. Nearly 230,000 people die. Family and friends I haven't heard from in months reach out to ask if I am okay.

On TV, the disaster is unfathomable. Entire lives, neighborhoods, and cities lost as thoughtlessly as though a child has kicked over a bucket of water and destroyed its own sandcastles.

8

Ishan and I meet in Bangkok or in India five times before we get married. In Thailand, I've become close to three other teachers I work with: my housemate Doris from Argentina, who teaches ESL, a confident and clear-headed woman with a sarcastic streak who makes great pasta salads; Sonya from Oregon, who teaches theology and world religions, whose mind I love to listen to when she asks big questions without worrying about answers; and Kung, our Thai friend who's just completed her doctorate in biology and is responsible for so much of our experience of real Thai culture. When I tell them about Ishan, all three of them are equally curious and worried. Can I trust someone I've rarely met? But when you're cooking dinner with friends, talking about people who matter to you, pushing each other the way good friends do, they listen.

I am the one who proposes to Ishan over the phone, soon after my Christmas visit to India. We begin to make plans and everything propels us toward the wedding. Ishan comes back to Thailand in May and we get engaged and legally married within a week, with the wedding ceremony to take place in August. By now, it's been a little over a year since we first met in Bangkok on my birthday.

In the meantime, he gets baptized as a Seventh-day Adventist because that's what I am, and because the school I work at won't allow someone to live on campus, even if married to one of the faculty, unless the person is baptized.

"Are you sure you want to do that?" I ask.

"I want to be with you, Ani. It doesn't matter what I have to do. If they need me to get baptized to move in with you, I will get baptized. Besides, I love your God. He listens to you."

He takes several Bible classes with a theology professor at Asia Pacific International University and I attend a few of those sessions, too. I like that Ishan asks questions and challenges the pastor's answers. I have never seen anyone in church, there or in the States or in Albania, do that. I am proud of him.

Soon after, my parents arrive from the States for the wedding. It is the first time they meet Ishan in person. His parents arrive from India the next day. We have put them up at a campus guesthouse where they have adjoining apartments. We take them around the campus, and to see where the wedding will take place. A few days later, we go to our wedding rehearsal together and that same evening to dinner at a resort where my mother says she has eaten the best fish of her life. Our parents get along well and seem to find similar points of interest, mainly hospitality—taking turns to make sure the other side has had enough to eat. Ishan's parents pay for one of the meals and for a tour we will take together on the Chao Phraya River after the wedding. In both Albanian and Indian cultures, it is a tradition to honor each member of the family by bringing gifts for each of them. My mother loves what Ishan's mother has picked for her—a Kashmiri house robe and a jacket, both handmade and colorfully embroidered on black wool. Our parents genuinely seem to like each other. Over a decade later, my dad will say of Ishan's mother, "She was happy seeing the two of you together. You could tell from her body language."

Of course, we haven't given them much of a choice. The wedding is happening. Everything is arranged. The flowers, the ceremony, the food, all paid for by me and by Ishan, and cooked by the cafeteria staff at the university.

The night before the wedding, Ishan discovers his suit pants don't seem to have a straight line running down the middle.

"I can't iron. You iron this. If you can't get a straight line I'm done with this. Fuck it. I'm not getting married."

I feel as if my heart and lungs leave my body. "What?" is all I manage, trying to convince myself that what I just heard really did come out of his mouth. "I can iron them," I say.

"If you fuck up and make them look shiny, I'm not going out there like that. I'm not going to embarrass myself."

"I'll ask my mom to iron them. She's much more careful than I am, okay? Just don't worry," I say.

This is all wrong. I know inside my body that it is. The way I hold back tears, the way I try to soften the knot I feel hardening at my throat. There is a conflict between my actions and what I know I need to do. But I march ahead to keep up appearances.

And why doesn't he ask his own fucking mother to iron his pants? Oh, right, she doesn't have her servants here with her. I am learning this new language with Ishan. The more intense he gets, the more I curse and protest in silence, but out of my mouth comes only, "I'll fix it, okay?"

It is near midnight and my mother irons the pants. She gives me a look that says, "What are you doing to yourself?" but the look doesn't offer me a way out. I take the pants back to Ishan, then slip into my bed like a shadow trying not to make noise for fear I will puncture my own dream. I take a two-hour nap and then wake up to get ready.

On this night, and against her instincts, my mother lets me exercise my own free will. She lets me have what I want. She doesn't try to stop the wedding, or make a scene. Maybe she has given up, knowing how strong-willed I am. Maybe, for once, she allows me to take my own risks, make my own mistakes.

9

Our wedding takes place outdoors at 7:00 a.m., partly to avoid the August Thai heat and the possibility of rain, which never fails to fall later in the day this time of year. But also partly because it is our wedding. Why does it need to be just like everyone else's? Instead of having my father walk me down the aisle, I ask both of my parents. I feel excited, but worried about them. My father forgets his tie, so we have to go back to my apartment for him to put it on.

In all the pictures of me walking toward Ishan, both my mother and father hold me by my elbows like a convict in court, unsmiling. My mother's face is unusually puffed up like she has slept for centuries and suddenly woken. My father doesn't raise his head or smile until I'm finally in front of everyone and he delivers me to Ishan.

Ishan and I have planned the ceremony together. The design and words on the wedding invitations, the material to make my gown and his suit, the flower arrangements. I have selected all the music we both love, which song will play when, who will walk when and how and where, what type of food will be served for breakfast. And yet some things are done exactly as they're done at weddings like this one—my father delivering me to Ishan as if all his life's purpose had been to someday do this one gesture for his daughter. This walk from the car to the place where Ishan and the pastor are waiting for me is punctuated by a mood of surrender rather than joy, a sort of muted shame rather than unconditional support on my parents' faces.

At the end of the ceremony, Ishan and I do this old Albanian tradition where we're supposed to release two white doves into the air. I hold on to mine, then open my hands and lift the bird up with both hands to let it fly off. Ishan holds on to his, then chucks it with one hand like throwing a frisbee.

After the wedding, we go home to change and quickly load all my boxes from the old apartment into a van and move to the other side of campus, up and down stairs to the third floor. That takes several hours. When the move is over, we shower and finally head to the city to meet up with our parents. We take them on a boat tour of Chao Phraya River, then visit the Reclining Buddha and Wat Phra Kaew, the temple of the Emerald Buddha. It feels good to watch our parents walking together, talking, taking pictures with everyone, telling jokes.

A relative of Ishan's lives in Bangkok and takes us all out that night. We eat on top of a skyscraper. A tall, famous singer in a bright red dress sings "At Last" and dedicates the song to us. When we go back to the hotel, we crash.

In some inarticulate way Ishan was Albania to me, a country I had feared because there were parts of it I didn't understand, and yet I loved it because it knew me in my childhood. There was a stubbornness surrounding my decision to marry Ishan, something of an "I'll show you all." But aimed at what? At whom? Who was I trying to convince?

On our honeymoon in Koh Samui, we go straight to bed, Ishan already hard, ready to enter me.

"Go slowly," I say.

"I am," he says.

We are not kissing or touching. We're focused on this one act. Penetration. He thrusts once and it feels like a sharp knife gutting me. I'm bleeding, already crying from the pain. He is concerned. I see it in his face.

"It's okay," he says. "We don't have to do this now. I love you." He kisses me.

"I love you," I repeat, like trying a password that will open doors, that will relax our bodies. But neither of us has that kind of faith. As soon as he tries to enter me, my mind says *no* and my body clenches. I feel mortified afterward, embarrassed and hurt, dysfunctional. It has to be my fault, I think. I'm too tense. This is supposed to work in this one simple way—he goes in. Why can't he get in? It never occurs to me then that there is no one simple way to have sex as movies and books have had us believe, and that, in fact, there's such a thing as bad sex. That we are both bad at it. Or that neither of us thought to take our time. And there is something else, too.

Part of me doesn't want to be entered, doesn't want to have inside me this man who himself is half-boy, half-violent, at times altogether unknown. What if I get pregnant? I don't want to have children with him. I fear he will hurt them.

The next day we drive all over the island, eat lunch near the ocean, swim in the pool at the resort where we are staying, check out gift shops. In the evening, we dine at the resort, then drive out to a liquor store to get some wine coolers. On the drive back, Ishan has one hand on the steering wheel and starts fingering me with the other. I've never felt so turned on by him. We can't wait to get back to our room. We walk up the stairs kissing each other, taking off our clothes. He wants to enter me again and . . . nothing. It hurts. He can't get in at all.

"You're like a wall," he says.

I don't know how many times we try that night or all ten nights we are there. It always ends with me crying, which is sometimes my body's way of telling me I'm being dishonest with myself. I don't want to have sex with him. I don't tell him that. What will it do to the marriage? Will he think I had lied about loving him? I put my body through one trial after another, to no avail. When he holds me and says it will be okay, I cry because he doesn't know I don't desire him and I don't know how to have that conversation. We fall asleep and the next morning, in the new sunlight, things feel new again, different. We will figure it out. He is understanding and will not push me, but we are both concerned that we don't seem to know how to get through this together. At times we don't even feel like trying. We conclude that loving each other will be enough. And maybe that I should see a doctor.

Two gynecologists, one in Thailand and later one in New Jersey, tell me I should drink some wine and try again.

"You are very lucky to have this man in your life," both doctors say, referring to his patience. I believed them. But now I wonder, what exactly were they suggesting? That it would have been understandable if he had forced himself inside me because I was his wife?

After seeing the Thai doctor, after trying so many times and getting nowhere, intimacy begins to feel like a chore and I do not bring it up anymore, with him or anyone else. I am more afraid of how he will react than trusting of the relationship, than checking in on how he is dealing with all of this. When we're alone, our hands get restless with our bodies and our bodies whir.

In Puri, India, we visit the Konark Sun Temple.

"How could these fuckers do this?" he says, laughing, as we walk by erotic carvings outside the temple. "This is what you should be doing with your husband, you *pidh*!"

"Really? Or maybe I should be doing this with Bhama, you *gaandu*!"

"Oooh, fine by me! Unë dua ty shumë tani, tani!" he says in his cute, broken Albanian, meaning he loves me very much right now. He hugs me tightly. *Uuuff!*

We travel all the way to Darjeeling with his parents and brother on a week-long vacation—a gift from his parents who belong to a Rotary Club. We get to stay for free at a beautiful hotel near Keventer's where you can sit on the terrace and eat a large plateful of delicious varieties of salami, sausages, and eggs for breakfast, hot coffee in your hands and the cool, crisp mountain air cupping your cheeks. The town's streets ribbon in spirals below you and the white range of Kanchenjunga mountains open wide in the distance. I have always seen mountains as the most generous of landscapes. You stand on them and they give you the world.

On our way to the Himalayan Zoological Park, locals stop me and ask me to wear a colorful traditional

We came to Darjeeling like cats at dawn
taking one curious step before the next.

The houses down below, inarticulate under fog.

When they heard our questions, monkeys
crawled out from behind the ruins, their gray bodies
etching on yellow walls, one arm's stretch
slowly after another. They made a little music,
the way they entered in and out of the morning.
We kissed. We held hands. In a way,
we've never left.

dress and a tea basket on my back for pictures. Ishan's parents tell me to agree, and they pay for it. On one of our afternoons there, Ishan takes me for a long walk around the grounds of his old school, St. Paul's. We walk forever, it seems, past the school's soccer fields, past St. Andrew's church, and then away, through alleyways and people's backyards, deep inside the town, away from the tourist center, all the way inside a little hole in the wall that seems to be no more than someone's living room. We sit at a tiny little square wooden table and the woman inside cooks us two bowls of spicy Maggi noodles and this particular meal at such a place makes my day. It's one of Ishan's favorite meals in Darjeeling. It is so simple to make, so packed with flavor, so he shares it with me.

Another night we go out to eat at an expensive restaurant and Ishan starts drinking. I don't remember how much; it doesn't seem like a lot. Back at the hotel, we hang out with his parents and Ishan continues to drink. When we get to our room, he's still drinking from the wine bottle and when we're in bed, it's too late. He's moaning. He's so loud. I don't sleep all night.

Ishan doesn't work while we're in Thailand. He is studying to complete a long-distance bachelor's degree in business administration with a focus on advertising. He travels every three months to India to take exams until his graduation in two years' time.

Our married life is adventurous at first. Ishan teaches me how to bike. We go on long rides starting early in the morning. Once, we bike forty miles on the highway, then exit somewhere that lands us at a Buddhist monastery. The early morning sun bathes the white streets, surrounding it in soft gold. At another corner, stray dogs chase us. And farther, for lunch, we discover a farm-to-table steakhouse. There is pleasure in planning fun things together. Sometimes that translates into us taking our bikes into the small town of Muak Lek to buy groceries, which we carry in our backpacks. I am grateful that Ishan carries so much more, his bag so full along the length of his entire back. After shopping, we stop at a Malaysian Muslim restaurant to have yellow rice with chicken and a spicy sweet-and-sour dipping sauce with caramelized crispy onions. His eyes light up when he eats this meal. I feel like flying, seeing him happy, because he often isn't.

We also stop for wine coolers from time to time, which both Ishan and I like, though I hurry him to pack them in his backpack in case we run into someone from school.

On the way home, he takes a shortcut that winds through hills and woods. The ride is bumpy and he takes off on the hills. I don't tell him how much it annoys me to be left behind because biking is one of few things that bring him joy. And

A long boat slices through the River Kwai. Water stitches itself right back.

as much as I love going with Ishan on these rides, he is often angry. Maybe I fall, or I lag behind, or one of his tires gets punctured. I offer to help or suggest an alternative solution, and he almost always responds with, "Shut the fuck up. You know nothing."

Later he'll apologize and say: "Stop being so scared, Ani."

10

I have had anxiety for as long as I can remember, though I could never name it. I imagine the worst outcome in a situation, before even trying. Entire years and tragedies unspool in my mind in the span of a few seconds before I even get to know someone. What they now call catastrophizing. Sometimes, I laugh about this. I'm Seinfeld. I'm Larry David. When I say no to anything Ishan suggests we do, he says I am simply being illogical or afraid. But why doesn't it ever occur to him that his joys aren't necessarily mine, and I don't need to participate in everything he wants to? Why doesn't it occur to me to say as much? Or maybe it does and I don't mention it because I am already becoming afraid of his reactions.

In December, we travel back to his parents' home in Kesinga to have a small Indian wedding with all his closest relatives attending. Imagine a wedding ceremony in which you are alone and everyone else attending is from the other person's family. This doesn't bother me at this time, but when I look at videos and photos of this day, I see a girl who looks happy, in awe of all the rituals and the colors, feeling loved by those people, yet she looks like a tourist. Not a bride. Not a lover. Not a wife. Not exactly someone's closest friend. Not exactly part of a family.

I enjoy the pre-nuptial games. In one, Ishan and I dip our hands into a big bowl of milky water with rice and look for the ring. I end up finding it and his grandpa laughs, christening me head of household. Then there is the one where you reach into a pan full of mustard seeds and press your fingers to them to see how many seeds stick to you. My hands are sweaty. I pick up a bunch and everyone laughs, half joking, half wishing for us to have that many children.

India runs away the
moment I arrive
but when I have to leave,
she gathers at my feet—
a monsoon that won't let
go, a capricious child.

But I am sharing all this with strangers. Yes, I know Ishan and his parents, brother, grandfather, and one of his aunts and her family, but everyone else I have only met this weekend. This is how my parents must have felt at our wedding.

At night, sitting by myself by the fire out in the yard while everyone is cracking jokes or talking and drinking, one of his

69

aunts comes and asks me to dance. If you could see this group of people from above, this one house full of women in beautiful saris of all colors around a fire, while outside the house there's a quiet village in the dark, and outside the village a darker, stranger land. Can you see that girl at all? Just a red dot in the dark—can you say she is truly there?

I admire my mother-in-law. She is strong and independent and I get the feeling that if she weren't around, this house would fall apart, weeds would grow, walls would crumble in a matter of days. Ishan often brags that she taught him all the English grammar rules, that she was a great teacher. She was one of the first women in her town to learn how to drive when she was young and studied French in high school. Ishan says that his father liked her because she was independent. They didn't have an arranged marriage. They fell in love. In pictures of the two of them, young, you can see in Ishan's dad's eyes that he adores her. They are quieter now, more weighed down with responsibilities perhaps. I don't know what it's like to be a businessman, your own boss, and manage people. Ishan's mother worked in her husband's U-bolt manufacturing company for years. When I visit the factory and meet some of the workers, I get the sense she knew how to run things there, that she is missed.

As I sit with her, she tells me of Hindu gods as if they are next-door neighbors she grew up with.

"The mother goddess takes many forms," she says, "but my favorite is Durga, I tell her everything." She says she never buys statues or portraits unless the painted eyes and smile show benevolence. "You must be comfortable with the way your gods look," she says. "What do you see when you pray, Ani, do you have an image of God in mind to focus on?"

"I must have some image," I say, "otherwise where's the connection?" Then I'm silent for a while. How can I tell her that I really don't have a face I relate to, that when I pray, I struggle not to think of what I have to do next or how I forgot to carry out this or that task. How can I tell her that there is simply a void, that only sometimes, when I most mean it, God takes the form of my prayer. I tell her it's funny how nothing exists unless we call it out or name it. She nods, carefully dusting Durga's face.

She and her husband are both religious and their devotion reminds me of my grandmother. They do *pujas* regularly—early morning prayers in the shrine room where they read from the Vedas scripture and listen to hymns in the background. My father-in-law, a tall, strong man with a soft, lovely voice, sings:

> *Tan man dhanjo kuch hai, sab hi hai tera.*
> *Tera tujhko arpit, kya laage mera.*

His voice overtakes the conversations in the other rooms. I ask Ishan to translate what he is saying.

> Mind, body, or wealth, whatever there is, it's already yours.
> I give you back what's yours, God, nothing belongs to me.

This sticks with me, becomes my line. It is me in this land, in this house, in this family, with all the lives I had

71

lived before, no longer mine. I let go of everything so I can take all of this in.

I love India with a child's curiosity. This country opens for me the moment I overcome an initial bout of anxiety. It opens and keeps opening, one layer after another, like a lotus flower in time lapse. I don't want to close my eyes. In some strange way, it's as if I'm in Albania again. Back in the late eighties, discovering so many things at once—first athletic shoes, first pair of jeans, first nail polish, first lipstick, first watch, first perfume. Who can keep count? Each discovery opens into another. Walking through Kolkata street markets, scents of cardamom or cumin hijacking my memories, trying to dodge a puddle of urine, or soot-stained aluminum pots in a street corner where an old man is shaving off a young one's beard—in India, everything is amplified. Saturated. The way the scent of jasmine takes over an entire room at night even though the plant is outside on the balcony. People grounded in and attached to the present; someone eating from a bowl with their fingers can teach you that. The past and the future have no weight the moment your fingers gather a mouthful of flavored rice and vegetables. You are where food is about to nourish you.

In India, there's a name for you. What you are named depends on who is calling for you.

Your brother-in-law calls you Bhabi. Your parents-in-law: Bhibi. Your husband has a name for you, too, although you call each other by many others. Your real name seems to sink somewhere, lower, like a heavy pendant behind a silk shirt. On

I cover a yellow hibiscus
in dirt by the railroad.
I wear bangles and a bindi
and at night I let my mirror wear it.

evening walks, my footsteps sound
something like a password I have
forgotten, but the only thing I can
access is the smell of the jasmine

in the garden after the dogs have been fed and chained away and
the door bolts turned down. I have family here. I am alone here.

GIRLHOOD

11

I SIT AT MY DESK trying to remember the last time the teacher called my name, hoping I'm safe for another week or so. I am in the second or third grade. They call us according to where our names fall on the alphabetical roster and my name ensures that I am always one of the first, if not always the first, to be called in front of the whole class. For years, through elementary school, middle, and all of high school, we are told to get up in front of the class and recite the day's assigned chapter.

I don't remember when my hands start to sweat, but I remember the day a teacher asks me to get up and recite a history chapter, the subject of which I no longer recall. I stand in front of the class panicking that my classmates will see the sweat building up on my palms. They're so wet that I can't think of anything else. What must they be thinking as they watch the little bubbles of water forming on my fingers like condensation on a steamy bathroom mirror?

Drip, drop . . . I'm talking and a drop of sweat, a whole drop, falls to the ground! I can no longer control the sweating or hide it by closing my fists, or putting my hands in my pockets. Another drop. I'm turning into a faucet. They will all see! They will all know what a freak I am. No one will be my friend.

"Sit down, Ani," says Ms. Bardha, and I am shocked. It's as though the whole thing was in my head. I get back to my desk and my hands are dry. None of my classmates say anything.

But the anxiety I feel at school is nothing compared to what awaits me outside.

In all the years I walk to and from school, to and from the bread store or mini-market, I walk with my back hunched. I don't want anyone to notice I have breasts. I keep my eyes to the ground, convinced I will slip by, invisible. It's becoming more and more common for young women my age to be kidnapped and sold into prostitution. Everyone wants to get rich overnight, and in a patriarchal culture, women are at the bottom of the hierarchical chain. They are currency, given to their men, taken from them. Human trafficking is becoming the new economic normal in post-Soviet Eastern Europe.

In Albania in the nineties, after the fall of a fifty-year-long Communist regime that strips everyone of their identity, men in their twenties and thirties are hungry to align themselves with what they perceive as power. They hang together in packs, harassing girls and women wherever they appear. After decades of isolation, the country is finally opening up to the rest of the world, trying to catch up: Everyone wants cars, groceries, clothes, lots of other goods imported from abroad. The latest jeans, the latest Adidas, the latest sunglasses, the latest BMW, the latest girl who passes through

75

their collective vision. What are girls but objects for men to claim?

Indrit is a few years older than I am and the leader of a gang of boys who enjoy terrifying me. They live in a neighborhood a few blocks away from mine that I have to walk by to get to school. They know when I get out of school, and they make sure to be at the corner of a building at the exact time I will pass by, then jump out to startle me, yell things, or stop me from going any farther simply by asking me questions: "Where are you going? Where were you this morning? What's your name? What's the hurry?" It is a type of bullying mixed with verbal harassment, poking at my sleeves and elbows, that twists my stomach and makes me wish I were either dead or invisible, just so I could cross streets without them seeing me.

Once, they bring a long steel wire and as soon as they jump out at me, they surround and tie me up from head to toe as if I am a pole they are spinning ribbons on. I have no power. I am one against seven or eight boys. They are laughing and I am crying, wondering how they can laugh when they can see I am in pain. The wire scratches my face from my ear to my mouth. When I tell my teacher, pointing at the red line on my face, what the boys did to me, led by Indrit, her student, she says, "Anuuush! He probably likes you. I will talk to him." But the next day, and the day after that, they come over to my building, under my balcony, at a time when they know my parents are at work, and yell, "Come out, Freya, come out!" Freya, the mysterious ghost character in the BBC drama miniseries

Maelstrom, popular on TV. Finally, I tell my father, and he finds out where Indrit lives. He tells Indrit's parents this has to stop. It finally does. I resolve to never let another guy on the street touch me again.

12

I am twelve when a classmate and I rush one morning to a new school after a gang burned ours down. She suggests taking a shortcut through an alleyway between two buildings. There is a young boy there—he could not be more than three or four years older than we are. He looks fierce, angry. He has a stick in one hand. It is the first time I feel it, a guy peeling himself from the landscape to approach me. He walks steadily, slowly, measuring the distance as he moves, but to me it feels as though he storms toward us. He asks, "What are you doing here?" My friend escapes under one of his open arms, but I get caught by the other. He shoves me up against the wall. His eyes move, full of rage, his teeth half-eating his own lips.

All I hear, all I hear even now, is him saying, "Hmm? Hmm?" as in, "You like this? Hmm? You like it?" as he rapes me right there against the concrete wall, in full daylight, each jab of his fingers trying to break open another wall. I don't know how he gets past my underwear. He disappears as quickly as he appeared. I am bawling. Someone yells from a balcony, "Girl, are you okay?" but I don't look up. I go straight to school.

For twenty years, I tell no one that this happened. In fact, it takes another ten years for me to realize he was probably part of Indrit's gang, sent to teach me a lesson after my father made it clear to him not to touch me.

Why, like so many other girls and boys who've had their bodies broken into, do I not tell anyone what happened? I have come up with answers to this question countless times. *Because it is quick. Because he doesn't take my clothes off. Because I don't die. Because I have no idea who he is. And isn't he still a boy himself? Because he doesn't do to me what I know can happen to girls. Because I'm good at holding things in. Because he touched me when I promised myself I wouldn't let a stranger do that to me. Because it is my fault for taking that shortcut.*

A few years later, I am turning a corner with my mother at the farmer's market in Tiranë when we find ourselves a few feet behind Tina, one of my neighborhood friends. She is walking with a man twenty years older than she is. He is holding her by the elbow. The way he holds her elbow looks like he's pushing her toward another street.

My mother doesn't like how this looks. You can see it in the way her face distorts like she smells something bad.

"Let's catch up," she says, "ask if she's okay. What's that man doing here with her?"

But I know Tina likes walking on her own. What if this is her boyfriend? What if we're reading too much into that hold? Tina and I are sixteen. I don't want my friend to think my mother is all up in her business.

"No, that's her uncle," I lie. "They're probably walking home."

Later that same afternoon, I find all my friends at Tina's door. There is Tina standing like something dangling from a clothes hanger. The girls say something about underwear, blood. She's crying. Then she goes inside, closing the door in a way that says she won't come out anymore. I say nothing to no one. At home, my mother looks at me again like she smells something bad, like saying, *I told you we should have stopped her*. All this before the lights go off in Tina's place, before I pull up the blanket, thinking perhaps we really could have helped, perhaps there was no point in doing that anymore. Hadn't Orsida's cousin a month earlier had a lavish wedding and been married off abroad only to find out soon after that her "husband" had sold her off as a prostitute?

Albanians describe the eighties and nineties as a time when *çunat ngacmonin gocat*, which means "the boys teased the girls." That choice of verb—*ngacmoj*, to tease—trivializes and removes responsibility from what happened. Even the word *çunat* (boys) doesn't accurately describe who was trespassing on whom. They were not all boys. There were plenty of grown men among them, in their twenties and thirties. For decades since, people have refused to name it for what it was. It was sexual harassment. There was sexual assault. Human trafficking. This was rape culture: when people consoled each other by measuring degrees of violence, by saying, "At least it wasn't rape. At least your daughter wasn't kidnapped." We go on enduring, instead of acknowledging that something is wrong and putting a stop to it.

When Communism finally crumbles, there is a lull for a brief moment, brief enough for you to open your eyes, as though you'd lived in darkness, turn your head, and see for the first time what has cracked apart all around you. The quiet before you hear the hyenas' cackling grow louder and louder in the distance and then, too late, you're surrounded, their roar smothering you from the inside out before they move to chew on your flesh.

The aftermath of a dictatorship is not freedom, unity, prosperity. There's mayhem first. And in Albania, young women pay the highest price.

13

We're a group and we share one identity: girls. We walk to school in our uniforms with a jean jacket or sweater on top. Always, we walk each other home. In one photo, we hug and lean on one another, evergreens behind us cut out of the frame. Sonila's laughter wakes the neighbors. My hair is short. It stays that way till I'm eighteen, move to another country, learn another language, and finally grow it out.

My friends and I plan routes walking to and from home together. "We can't go that way," we say, "that's where the guys *gjuajnë gocat*" (hunt the girls). It's as if all the humans have suddenly transformed into a new breed of animal. We, the girls, are the zebras. They, the boys, are the hyenas: in packs, by the school wall, standing at apartment corners. How do you avoid them? How do you survive their attacks? Especially when they seem to multiply like colonies of lice. They have their eyes on us. The idiom is exactly the same in Albanian: *ja vuri syrin asaj* (he placed his eye on her). Or the equivalent: *ja qepi syrin* (he stitched his eye on her). Like a mark, we carry those eyes on our backs, on our chests, on our faces, and deep within. We are not our own. When you are watched, when you are hunted, you thin out. Then you're gone.

My high school years can be summed up by the experience of walking back and forth to school with my best friend, Alda. Forget the learning that took place. What rises to the surface is the constant uncertainty of the safety of those streets, how we walk everywhere together.

Her house is ten minutes away from mine. Each morning I look out from my balcony to see if she is getting closer and then we walk together for another twenty minutes until we reach the school. My heart sinks each time I don't see Alda on the horizon by a certain time. It means she is sick and won't be coming and I have to walk alone.

On our walks back home, she often asks me to accompany her for another five minutes, or sometimes all the way to her place so she won't have to deal with ambushes. When girls walk alone, they are vulnerable. If they have one or two friends along, they are rarely messed with. But what will I do to get home after dropping her off?

"Come on, Ani, just five minutes. You don't have to come all the way. Besides, look, there's nobody out here now. And nobody will mess with you," she adds, ruffling my short tomboy hair.

I go. Sometimes I reach the five-minute mark and she begs me to go with her a little farther and I can't say no. Then I walk the ten minutes home alone repeating in my head, *t'qifsha robt, t'qifsha t'gjithë robt* (fuck everyone, fuck them all), my hands digging deep inside my pockets making fists, releasing them, making fists again to the rhythms of a beating heart.

I know I will have to accompany Alda.

I know I will have to walk home alone.

I know someone, or more than one guy, will then stop me.

I know I will not let them touch me.

I know I will eventually get home.

I don't know, each time, how much harder it is becoming to see myself. I am the most unpredictable thing around me.

As a teenager, I spend many summer evenings walking to and sitting on the Piramida, which is a twenty-minute walk from my house. Piramida, otherwise known as the Pyramid of Tiranë, was built in 1988 as a museum dedicated to the legacy of Enver Hoxha. After the collapse of the Communist regime, the Pyramid ceases its original function, becomes an expo and conference center by day, and a playground for kids and teenage trysts by night. I climb up to the top and slide all the way down using my butt as a sled. Afternoons, girlfriends from my neighborhood and I walk to the Pyramid, sit and chat, and are joined by a band of boys we know from a neighborhood next to ours. We share

On rainy days, we'd go to
   Xhilda's place:
me, Elona, Jonida, Fiori.
   Xhilda had a balcony.
We'd go out there and talk to
   the boys.

Xhilda lived on the first floor.
So we could touch hands with
   the boys.
Except the balcony had iron
   bars because

you must protect yourselves
   from thieves.
So we could touch hands with
   the boys
with bars touching ours.

a smoke, and some of us kiss, a little distanced from the rest. But I never did. Those few days I see myself briefly—I recognize my happiness is real, something tangible, measured by the long hours surrounded by friends as the skies darken and the stars come out, enjoying our time together swapping stories, listening at the edge of our senses to something like desire spark.

Who am I if I slip from one street to another, never making eye contact with anyone? I don't have an adolescence. I erase it.

Except for the year I am seventeen. I save money and buy a pair of army-brown jeans that I love. I buy combat boots. I wear makeup because I want to. My friend Elona teaches me how to apply mascara: "First, close your eye," she says, "then use the brush to lift the eyelashes up—don't open your eye! Keep lifting upward, then sideways toward the outer corner. Now open your eye. Now brush the bottom ones. Look at those broom-length lashes!"

I love my style. My suit of oxblood-plaid short pants and vest is my favorite. I wear it with tights and a white shirt and know it's going to make me stand out. I wear it anyway. I want to be noticed. To be seen by someone for who I am. My best friends have boyfriends. I don't. I am a girl wanting a boy to see me. And so, in small ways, I try to be myself, choosing what I want to look like, choosing what to wear.

I even put highlights in my hair, just a few caramel streaks. I look like a cute skunk and I feel strong. Being a girl or a woman, you learn to equate strength with simply feeling comfortable in your own skin.

One morning a policeman who works at the French embassy notices me. He stops me on my way to school, pulling me toward the embassy's wall.

"Who do you think you are?" he asks, gripping me by the wrist. "Coloring your hair like that?"

He is maybe twenty years older than I am. I didn't think I needed to ask his permission.

"I have to go to class," I say, trying to raise my voice a little so he'll understand I'm concerned about school.

But I can hardly finish my sentence before he slaps my face so hard it burns. I realize I have no one to protect me here. No one. That's all I can think about. *No one* suddenly magnifies and becomes the country I live in. I live in *NO ONE*—a place where there is no help when you most need it, no love to believe in. I start to cry. The cop lets me go.

When I get to class, my friends ask me what happened. They can see I've been crying.

When I tell them, they say that the cop has the hots for me.

After I tell my mother, she goes to talk to the cop the next morning. In a small country, there's a blessed curse: in every city or town, everyone knows everyone, and my mother knows his boss. She tells the cop she'll get him fired if he ever lays a hand on me or other girls again.

All I ever want is to stop being watched. It's as though a mirror is always with me—I cannot see myself but instead this self that is constantly watched by others, constantly stopped. This is when *silence* becomes a language I learn to be proficient in.

I consent nothing to no one. I learn to live like a punctuation mark, a comma, arriving *after* each phase of my life. I choose to never be *in* my teens. I choose to be *delayed*, *absent*, until my teens have left me.

I never have a boyfriend in Albania. When I leave the country at eighteen, *boy* and *man* are still synonymous with someone watching me, much like the government and the secret service watched our parents' every move for decades. Are these the same boys who played hide and seek with us, with whom we touched hands through a balcony's iron bars when they called us to come out and play? The boys with whom we shared stories, long after sunset, sitting along a wall like a small army, trying to protect what we couldn't know was about to be snatched away? They are, and they aren't. Up until 1988, when the Albanian Communist regime begins to fall apart, these boys are our friends. Then, as if overnight, they are gone, replaced by older, louder, angrier, hungrier ones who show up on the streets, patrolling corners, buildings, schools.

14

At seventeen, I skip school one day with two of my girl-friends. It's what everyone does. At some point it becomes uncertain if we will even graduate. So many school days have been canceled as people take to the streets protesting the government.

We have plans to go to the beach—me, Alda, Elona, and their two boyfriends. What I don't find out until we leave is that Elona's boyfriend, who was twenty-nine years old at the time, is bringing along another guy, also in his late twenties.

"It will be fine," Elona says enthusiastically. "He's a nice guy. He's seen you before. He'd like to just get to know you."

We take Alda's boyfriend's car and stop at a terrace café on the outskirts of town for a soda, which then turns into a beer and a couple of cigarettes. I can't smoke, don't know how to inhale. I just suck the smoke, hold it in my mouth, and blow it all out like I know what to do.

The culture is changing all around us. Where a few years ago you had to wait in line to buy bread, rice, milk, and other basic staples in the one supermarket of the neighborhood, now you can choose to go to any of the many stores available. There are no more lines. The only cars on the road used to be those of government officials, celebrities, or the police, which one could count on two hands, and now you have people like Alda's boyfriend who bought his own car before turning twenty. It's his entire business—chauffeuring passengers in and out of the city in all directions. He makes lots of money, or so it seems.

Where only a decade ago I made toast with a layer of sugar and green olive oil on top and was happy, now groceries beckon from foreign countries—Greece, Turkey, Italy, Serbia. There are sodas. I have my first Coke in my early teens. My first croissant filled with Nutella at fifteen. I try ice cream bars, chewing gum of all kinds of flavors, colors, and textures; a decade ago, if a single piece came my way by accident, I would chew it all day, and at night, I would faithfully deposit it in a glass of water. I could pick it up again and chew it through the next day. And wasn't

Bela the one who taught me that you could change the gum's color if you used your mother's lipstick on it? All her chewing gum was blood red. Where just a few years ago the only store and restaurant in the neighborhood were government-owned, now family-owned businesses, retail stores, supermarkets, little kiosks, bars, clubs, and children's centers have sprouted on each street like mushrooms after rain.

We sit on the terrace of a family-owned two-story-house-turned-local-café-bar having a drink, making small talk, anticipating the day ahead. We get up and drive straight to the beach, listening to cassette tapes of Italian bands I still listen to from time to time: 883's "Sei un mito," Luca Carboni's "Mare, mare," and "Ci vuole un fisico bestiale," among others, singing of what a beastly body you need to have to take the blows life deals you, a beastly body to drink and smoke, because we're always at a crossroads, we're boats in the middle of the ocean. The six of us are well-versed in Italian—nearly every Albanian, at least when I was living there, spoke and sang and breathed Italian through the TV, radio, and cassette tapes circulating among us. I studied it with a tutor for a year, but I think I truly learned it from all the Italian media accessible to me. We live and see our youth in the Italian broadcasts. My girlfriends and I know all the songs, imitate the hairstyles and clothing we see on *Non è la RAI*, a TV show that airs every day in the afternoons starring a hundred adolescent girls who dance, sing, and sell products. Imagine a country whose youth was only able to watch TV during the hours of 6:00–10:00 p.m. when the Albanian TV programs aired. Now suddenly we have

87

twenty-four seven access to dozens of channels from several European countries.

What is a cooped-up animal going to do the day you unleash him in an open field? This is when thousands of people begin to leave Albania. Some of us already have cousins and other relatives who left for Italy or other neighboring countries in the first mass exodus of 1991. Others dream of going there, too. Everyone wants to make a better life anywhere but here.

My friends and I ride with the windows down, blasting Carboni, singing along, "Sea, oh sea, I want so much to reach you, I'm speeding up and take you now . . . " I love this song, which is mainly about a young man leaving Bologna at night on a motorcycle, wind on his face, longing to meet the girl who's no longer with him—call it girl, call it sea, all the same.

I can feel it now, decades later, writing about this young girl. School is the last thing on her mind. Tasting something different, salt-scented, with sand between her toes, the possibility of finally being kissed . . . Maybe she is thinking of what it might be like to leave this country one day, what it must be like to move toward a different future. She must be dreaming of these things as they accelerate toward Durres, the beach town just outside the capital city.

When we reach the beach, we walk for a good while. We walk in pairs, my friends and their boyfriends and me and this guy who has tagged along because he wants to get to know me. At some point, I can't see my girlfriends anymore. It's April and the beach is empty. I am alone with this person whose name I don't remember. He tries a few times to kiss me, and even as I understand that he is interested in me, I realize I'm not attracted to him. He is too old and too tall and we don't have anything in common. He will only talk about my looks and ask me to smoke another cigarette, which I don't care for. We just walk until we're joined by the others.

We have lunch at a restaurant, then head home. The whole time, I know that it could have gone really badly. I've learned to live holding two realities at once: how safe I am and what the alternative could be.

When I get home in the afternoon, I'm standing in the corridor removing my shoes and find my mother looking furious, livid. It's as though she's been waiting to ambush me.

"Where were you today?" she demands, and I know right away that she knows I skipped school. Someone has told her. I confess. If she looked livid when I opened the door, she now looks entirely a stranger: lost in anger, madness, disappointment. She can't believe it, and won't accept it when I try to assure her that we just had lunch on the beach and nothing happened, that I didn't even like the guy.

It's over—I am never to hang out with this group of girlfriends again.

"But, Mom—" *I'm seventeen, when will you just let me make my own mistakes!?* I want to ask her. *You can't tell me who I can or can't be friends with*, I want to yell, but can't.

"Did you hear what I said?" she asks. "You're never to hang out with your friends again." Soon after, she storms out of the apartment.

My heart feels small, tight, painfully so. My own mother doesn't trust me. She has made a demand and means it.

I pick up my diary and start writing. These are friends I see in every class every single day. They are so much more than friends. We look out for one another in ways our parents aren't aware of. These are friends I share and live through fears with. How can I not talk to them? And what will they think of me then? Of my mother, of how controlling she can be? I get up and stand in front of the medicine cabinet. I take out a bottle of Grandma's Valium pills. I count fifteen of them, fill a glass of water, and swallow them all at once.

I take my diary into my parents' bedroom. On the way there I tell my brother—twelve years old at this time—what I have done. He freaks out when he sees my handwriting begin to change into giant, slow letters. Single words begin to take up their own pages.

When my parents return home, along with a couple of friends of theirs who are visiting for the evening, I am in the bedroom, nearly passing out. My brother tells my parents in the corridor after they've shown the guests into the living room.

"What have you done? What have you done to us?!" my mother yells at me in the bedroom, trying to keep her voice down. "We have guests! Don't you come into the living room. Do you hear me? Stay right here, I'll be right back."

As drugged as I am, I don't know where I find the strength to get up and walk into the living room, dragging my elephant-heavy legs. I think I want water. Or maybe I just want to show myself—messed up and all. Maybe I am trying to get back at my mother.

I feel that I am moving slowly and that I probably speak even slower. There's a thick noise, people mumbling around me, and the room is incredibly bright from the ceiling lamp. I guess the guests know now—Ani tried to overdose.

Look, even twenty years after the fact, I completely fail to name the act: I didn't try to overdose. I tried, quickly and clear-headedly, to kill myself.

"What has she done?" the man asks from the couch, and learns that I have taken Valium.

"Quickly, give her a glass of milk!" he urges my parents. My dad boils a cup and brings it over to me. It has formed that skin on the top that makes me churn when I see it.

"I don't want it, I don't like that it has that skin," I say, turning to my brother so he can grab the cup and save me from having to take it, but no sooner have I finished that sentence than my father slaps me across the face.

"Drink it!" he demands.

"Your head flew slowly to the left," my brother narrates days later, nervously laughing.

My dad hardly ever yells, let alone lays a hand on us. I drink it.

Soon after, we discover that the pills had expired, and the repercussions are not serious. I sleep for a long time, what feels like twenty-four hours, and then again, several hours off and on. The whole incident is swept under the rug. If I mention it in the years that follow, my mother stamps it out like a flame: "What's the point in recalling such things?"

I understand now that my mother is embarrassed by her response. She wishes she had done something differently. She wishes she hadn't cared what other people thought. Isn't she the same woman who, the day after I am born, wakes up from the anesthesia alarmed by the discovery that the hospital tag she expects to see around her wrist is no longer there? The wristband with my name and vitals on it. She screams at the nurses. She doesn't care at this moment what anyone thinks of her yelling with the full strength of her lungs: "Where is my baby? I want to see my baby! Bring me my baby now!" She will not calm down until one of the nurses brings me to the door, where we stay, because my mother has caught pneumonia.

After she sees me, she drifts peacefully to sleep. And then, when she wakes a little later, she feels something under her back, between her nightgown and the sheets, so she reaches behind her back to search, feels something hard and curled, and lifts it to her face. It is the wristband with her name, my vitals, and birth date on it.

"She's alive! My daughter is alive!" she shouts, and although I have never had children of my own, I can feel the joy she must know at this moment.

The first time she tells me about this day, she says: "You were not an easy birth. The umbilical cord was wrapped around your neck twice. I had to have a C-section—in Albania, in 1978. The doctors gave me more anesthesia than necessary and I caught pneumonia as a result."

We will spend three more weeks in the hospital before arriving home together.

I think I finally understand why she never wants to talk about my attempted suicide. I understand her fear of losing me, whether I'm a fetus inside her, a one-day-old, or seventeen. I know why she never wants to talk about this memory. It's beyond language to explain to someone you love how you never want to lose them. Yet, the actions you take to try to prevent that loss are just that—an attempt, even if you fail. The truth I know is that you never lose those you love. But what if you lived in a country where nothing belonged to you, not even your thoughts? What does it mean to have a child in a world like that, knowing you can't protect her from it all?

THE HALF-LIT CORNER

15

MY PATERNAL GRANDFATHER, Ligor, who died a few months before I was born, is a big part of the reason my family immigrates to the United States.

It's 1910. Industrialization is at its peak and America experiences a second wave of immigration, this time predominantly from southern and eastern Europe. At seventeen, Ligor leaves Albania for Italy. From there, he takes a ship to America and lands in Boston. Back home, only his mother, a young widow, remains; he is her only son. Ligor works various jobs in Concord, New Hampshire, but the winters are unbearably cold. Within a year, he and his friends take the train and relocate to Seattle.

I try to imagine this young man who is only a year younger than I will be when I move to Massachusetts. I will throw myself into my studies, wanting to perfect my English as he threw himself into work to send money home to his mother. There he is, on the train to Seattle, a tall, thin Albanian who makes everyone laugh with his endless jokes and stories, his hazel-blue eyes and blond hair everyone talks about, too young to care about his looks, unaware of the lives he has yet to create.

In Seattle, Ligor finds work at a steel factory for the Boeing Company. Years later, raising my father, he will tell him about the large buckets of hot, melted steel he carries daily with both hands from one end of the factory to the other. For decades, my father will keep Ligor's old leather wrist cuffs that he and the other workers wore while holding those heavy buckets so their wrists wouldn't snap.

Ligor's boss likes how hardworking he is and wants to make him his son-in-law. He offers to put him through school, but says that Ligor's pay will have to decrease. Ligor needs a certain amount of money to send home, so he turns down the offer and works hard for another ten years.

His mother sends letters asking him to come back and marry an Albanian girl. Somehow she arranges this before he meets his fiancée. Ligor plans to go home to get married, and then return to the U.S. with his new bride.

There is a photo of him sitting on a chair with his elbow on a table and his hand to his temple. Daisies in a vase on the table. He wears a clean black suit, white shirt, black leather shoes.

"You know why his hand is up to his temple like this?" my father asks me. He doesn't wait for me to guess. "The cameraman asked him to put his finger to his temple for the shot. He told him, 'Think again, Ligor, think twice before leaving this country.'"

In 1920, with a temporary American passport that is valid for one year, Ligor reaches Albania and marries the girl his mother chose for him. Unfortunately, as was happening to so many families at the time, Ligor's wife falls ill with tuberculosis soon after they marry. She dies within the year. In the process, all the money Ligor had saved in America helps to foot the hospital bills and medical treatments. Meanwhile, his temporary American passport expires.

A year later, he looks for a new wife and goes to see a man he respects. The only thing he has heard about the man's daughter is that she is seventeen. When my grandfather enters the man's house, he sees Meropi sitting on a stool on the patio, intent on reattaching the handle of a small coffee pot. He tells my dad this is why he immediately liked her—because she seemed to have the mind to be self-sustaining, trying to fix something rather than throw it away.

Meropi's father had already been asked for his daughter's hand by another man, "a filthy rich guy," as he describes him.

"You have two choices, Meropi," her father says. "Think carefully and choose wisely."

Meropi thinks and prays. She has no one else to advise her—her mother passed away when she was nine. Either the rich man who is known to be an alcoholic, or Ligor, who is hardworking, older by ten years, widowed, without any known vices, and mostly broke.

When my father says, "She chose Ligor," I think I see tears in his eyes.

I like the fact that my grandmother chose for herself even though in 1920s Albania she didn't have many choices to begin with.

Decades later, after Communism isolates Albania from the rest of the world, whenever Ligor drinks with his closest friends (some of whom he'd known in America), they toast: "May the roads and borders open again." He never stops wishing to come back, or at least to have his children come here, this country that promises freedom and the pursuit of happiness. Throughout his life, my father hears his father: "Do your best and try to get to America. Whatever you do, go to America."

16

In the course of their marriage, my grandparents are blessed with nine children, although only four live on to adulthood. Four die young, as babies, of scarlet fever or other diseases, and another, eleven-year-old Loni, dies when a drunk driver hits him while he is bicycling home. I don't know what it was like for my grandparents to lose all these children. By the time Loni dies, they have had seven and are left with two. I don't know how they bring themselves to even dream of another, but in 1944, Meropi gets pregnant again. A whole lifetime later, when she comes to live with my parents, to help raise me and my brother, she will tell me about this peculiar time in her life when nothing made sense, least of all God.

Meropi was raised Orthodox and so was my grandfather. She is now pregnant, but still mourning her eleven-year-old son. Many are the days when she will fast, praying to God for another son, and sure enough it is my father growing in her belly. A few years prior, she has been introduced to a protestant pastor,

Daniel Lewis, a Seventh-day Adventist Albanian missionary who studied in America and came back to preach in their town.

Daniel creates a small community of about eight or nine regular members who meet with him on Saturdays to study the Bible. Meropi can't get enough. It all makes sense to her—to study the Bible and discuss it with fellow believers, rather than only hear verses chanted in church as it is practiced in her Orthodox faith. If she feels she needs forgiveness, she can pray directly to God rather than confess her sins in the presence of a priest. One of the Seventh-day Adventists' core beliefs is in Jesus's second coming, and Meropi holds fast to that, the idea that our loved ones will be reunited with us again. But it is a time of war, and when the war ends, Communism swoops in and cracks down on all religions across the land. Government officials destroy churches and mosques and forbid worship of any kind. The only entities worthy of worship are the Communist party and its leaders. This is when my father is born. And my grandmother, who has just rediscovered God, is not about to give it all up. She and a few other friends continue to meet with their pastor in secret every Saturday—they gather at a different person's house each week so it doesn't look suspicious.

My grandmother wants Ligor to convert from Orthodox to Seventh-day Adventist, too. Ligor can see how much peace my grandmother has found in her new faith, and tells her she is free to believe whatever she wants, but he will remain Orthodox. But on his deathbed, decades later while the country is still atheist, he will ask Meropi to read the Bible to him because he trusts her faith more than his own.

Yet, in 1945, the small town of Korçë is no different from any other part of Albania—everyone begins to spy on each other. People soon catch wind of what Meropi and her friends are up to. Word gets to my grandfather when his own cousins nag him: "What's wrong with your wife? Is she a Jew now, keeping the Sabbath? How could you let her convert to Judaism?" One day he comes home and tells her, "If you don't stop this religious business right away, we are done."

They argue. Meropi won't change her mind, but to Ligor, as to so many Albanians, public opinion matters more than faith. And yet, he doesn't fully have it in him to tell her what to do. He resolves to ask the bishop in his Orthodox church to advise him. My grandmother will tell me that he gave her an ultimatum that day: "I'm going to get advice from the bishop. If he says you're not guilty and I should let you continue to practice this faith, then I will. But if he tells me you're wrong to follow this religion, then we're divorcing, so you should pack up your stuff and be ready to leave."

As my grandmother waits for Ligor to return and deliver his verdict, she wraps my five-month-old father in small, white cotton fabric, fastening the edges with safety pins. She wraps him, fastens him, then unfastens and unwraps him, trying to make up her mind whether to take the baby and leave, leave alone, or stay. It's December—snow and bitter wind envelop Korçë. What about her other children? Will she leave them behind? I never ask her. Her own parents have already passed away and she has no siblings. It would have been just Meropi and her God and I know she would have done it.

The bishop welcomes my grandfather and calmly explains how faith is like a pillar from the earth to the heavens and all the various religions embrace it at different heights. He lists which religion is at what height, and to my grandpa's surprise, the Orthodox religion embraces the pillar much lower than the Seventh-day-Adventist one. "They're a much stricter religion than ours," he tells Ligor, "worthy of more respect for their obedience toward God."

"Can you believe this!?" my grandma always asks when telling me this story. "This, coming from the Orthodox bishop! In Albania, in the nineteen forties! He had to have recognized something worthy in a religion that actively studies the word of God."

"So if you choose to divorce your wife, not only I, but God himself, will curse you," the bishop finally tells Ligor, and my grandfather never bothers my grandmother again about it.

I like to believe Ligor made this story up to silence his cousins and let Meropi do what she wanted when he recognized her conviction. I like to think he loved her for who she really was, that he would never impose on her, much less desert her, no matter what anyone else thought. But reality is much more complex and tragic. He really did worry about public opinion. And yet, wrapped up as he was in that conviction that wives should follow what husbands say, it didn't occur to him that what mattered most to Meropi was her own faith: she would put this before her marriage any day.

"He came home and told me: 'Fine, Meropi, do what you want about God from now on, just don't involve me in it!'" She finishes the story, a smile on her face—triumphant, proud.

She will keep her faith from then on, and my father will grow up learning about God and the Bible, praying and talking about God with his mother in the secrecy of their house, and sometimes even go with her to Pastor Stevens's secret religious meetings.

And in a few years, the authorities will discover these meetings and find a way to arrest Pastor Stevens when someone from Korçë betrays Stevens while he is trying to escape to Italy with his family. Pastor Stevens is sent to prison with his wife, their children sent to an orphanage. My grandmother visits them frequently in prison, does their laundry, brings them food. I don't know what happened to the other faithful members of the group, but since that day, my grandmother keeps the Sabbath and tithe savings all on her own.

I can't help but wonder how much of Ligor's blood—who he was and how he lived—runs in me. If he hadn't come to America in the early twentieth century, my family may have never thought to immigrate here. And if he'd never returned to Albania, we would not exist.

17

After a lot of thought, after making sure this is also what he wants, Ishan and I move to the U.S. We decide to live with my parents in Massachusetts until we can find jobs and our own place. It is Ishan's first time in America.

My mother has yet to accept Ishan. Every time she sees him, she seems to realize all over again that I did not accomplish what she must have envisioned for me—to marry someone financially stable with whom to buy a house, have good jobs, a child or two, and ultimately support her and my father when they get older. He feels this and resents her. One evening, in my bedroom we now share, he tells me he feels that I don't have his back. That I don't stand up for him to my mother. He yells at me. My mother hears and rushes into the room.

"Why are you yelling? Who are you, yelling at my daughter like that?"

"I'll yell if I want to. She's my wife."

"She's my daughter. This is my house."

"Then I will leave her. I don't give a shit. Fuck this!"

"Go. You can go right now!" my mother yells back.

Though I never saw my mother confront the policeman who harassed me in Albania, I have a sense now of what that must have been like.

"Stop!" I say and push her away. "Can you please leave us alone? We need to talk about this alone."

She is upset. He is upset. And I'm thinking: *What the fuck is this? How can you speak to my mother like that?* Will he ever be good enough for her? I say nothing, though, except: "Please, Ishan, don't be like this. She's just worried about me. She heard you yelling at me."

"I can yell at you if I want to. You're my wife. It's none of her fucking business. This is bullshit. I left my country for you, Ani. I left my home, a perfect job. I had servants. What about here? I have nothing. I'm nobody."

It hurts. I know all of this is true and hard for him. The marketing job he had in his father's business for two years before moving to Thailand was a stable, decent job. He hasn't adjusted to this new country yet, has found no work, no feeling of having a family. And yet. *Why are you talking about me like I am your property?*

The yelling stops after a while. Only a sense of something static lingers, like the low crackle of glowing embers once a fire starts to fade. Ishan and I fall asleep like I imagine twins or little best friends do, small and holding each other tight, or maybe holding the dream they've believed in so desperately that they look even smaller than themselves, the whole universe much darker and impossibly endless, wrapped around them.

A month later, Ishan finds a job in New Jersey as a marketing communications specialist. He hasn't gotten his license yet, so I drive a U-Haul truck over the George Washington Bridge with all the stuff we had shipped to my parents' place from Thailand. I have never driven that far before and wouldn't have done it if he hadn't pushed me. He is proud of me.

We move into a basement floor apartment, our windows overlooking the parking lot and people's feet, so we keep the windows closed and the shades down.

I find part-time lecturer positions in the Writing Program at Rutgers University and in the English Department at Kean University. We are finally somewhat financially independent again.

We make enough money to save a little. We cook. We go out. Things are exciting for a while, as they are when you move into a new environment, always discovering what's around every corner. Then a new person joins the company and Ishan starts drinking again now that he has a drinking buddy. He drank off and on throughout the time we were together in Thailand, and I saw it get bad once or twice before, when we visited India. He comes home one night late after work, one of his friends holding him up, delivering him to me at the door. He collapses, limp, on the bed.

The waitress seats us by a window,
where, left to ourselves, we feast on
foreign words, baklava, and honey wine
and you call me *patlican*.

Time eats the night and excretes the night.

As usual, I listen and your hands
dictate the theme of the conversation.

We are new to New Jersey—I hardly know anyone. All my friends are either back in Massachusetts or scattered in other states. Ishan has made an Indian friend he seems to get along with well, but Ishan has told me of him having hit his wife. I try to avoid him.

When Ishan starts drinking, I never once think it is his way of coping with a situation that has gotten out of his control. I don't seek help. Instead, I register it as him not caring about our marriage; by now, even though I have not thought or verbalized it to myself, I am beginning to not care about it either. The next day, he always apologizes, promising he will stop, that we will be better again. "Let's go out, Anu," he says. We go out for dinner, then come back to our apartment at the world's end, isolated from everything. Nobody visits us.

18

One morning, Ishan decides we should get a dog. A big one.

I didn't grow up with dogs but he did, German shepherds being his favorite, but now he prefers pit bulls. We look at profiles on websites. We go to a shelter in Bloomfield and I am immediately drawn to a black and white pit bull because he looks so happy. I ask to meet him. His name is Petey, and he's a year old, very energetic. They let him out of the cage to meet us and he is immediately taken with Ishan, who knows exactly how to play with him. They start a game of tug of war. Petey loves it. Starts growling. Having never had a dog before, I worry this means he is aggressive. "Nah, this is what dogs do," Ishan explains.

It is settled. I am a little apprehensive, but deep down I feel a sense of trust in this dog. I feel like I already know him.

"We want to adopt this one," we say.

"He's a stubborn one, returned twice," we are told. "The owners couldn't handle him. Are you sure you want him? This is his last chance."

We talk to a trainer at the shelter who agrees to help us out with some of Petey's behavior issues. The trainer says he can come to our house. We go to the shelter two more times to get to know Petey better, and learn how to walk him using a Gentle Leader headcollar. He is "one stubborn motherfucker," as Ishan calls him.

The day we take him home, we drive down Garden State Parkway with the windows down. Petey loves it. He'll always love car rides.

And he is a doll. No shoes chewed. Hardly any barking. No accidents, ever. Loves to play. Alert. Sweet. He challenges me sometimes, but I learn to teach him tricks, how to sit and wait for his food. He waits for the next command, eyes locked with mine, with that expectant, trusting look that says he knows food is coming but he'll be a good boy and wait perfectly for it until I'm ready.

Walking him, however, is a different story. It takes months and months and about $1,000 in training fees to get Petey to calm down. I fall on my face twice. I sprain both my knees when he decides to run after a squirrel I don't notice before he does, and it will be weeks before I can walk like myself again. Ishan starts drinking again, and most nights he decides he is not going to take the dog out.

We've made a home again
and the government wants proof
our marriage is genuine.
We don't know our neighbors.
We don't love more than a dog.
In bed, at night, we're still shy
and broken like children.

I am afraid of your silence,

the moment after the glass has broken,
the second before I realize that car will crash

I am afraid of starting something—

my hands are like two continents
swimming farther and farther off the map.

"You do it."

I do it. That is me: walking Petey at night, looking at the empty black sky wondering what the fuck I am doing with this life.

In January, I decide to apply to the graduate MFA program in poetry at Boston University, the only program I can find with a March application deadline. I want to get back to my writing. I also want to move back to Massachusetts, where I have always felt at home.

Early in April, I get a call from a Boston area code: they offer me a full ride.

The news excites us both. Maybe Ishan can keep his job and work from home and drive to New Jersey once a week or so. It's a good idea, though it won't last. We drive up to Boston one weekend to check out places and settle on a two-family house in Framingham. Ishan tells me that as soon as he met the landlord, Jim, a landscape artist, and saw that he was wearing two different shoes, that settled it for him. I feel the same way when I meet the landlady, Linda, who works as a special-ed teacher; after touring the apartment, I have a feeling that something is going to end in this house, yet it's a positive, intuitive sense. I trust it.

The apartment is full of windows. An 1840s house, with an ancient cemetery in the backyard, creaking doors, floors, and old windows that let in a draft. But the rent is very cheap and heat is included. They have a big black lab named Burton. We have our big Petey. They love ours right away. We move in.

I couldn't have known it then, but applying to the poetry program was my way of looking to get out of my marriage.

Words have always told me what I didn't yet know or wasn't ready to accept.

Our landlord has a son named Max who comes home from college every holiday and parties with his old high school friends from the neighborhood. One night, they are drinking in the back-yard and Ishan joins them. Next thing I know, Jim is bringing Ishan upstairs

*You sit with your right
hand pressed
palm-down on your desk
as if to calm a dog,
your left searching your
pocket for a cigarette.
If Hopper could have
painted us,
I'd be the half-lit corner.*

and I hear that he has bitten Max's ear. I try to get him to go to bed, but he gets up and heads for the kitchen. He pisses on the cabinets by the sink, probably thinking he is in the bathroom. When he realizes his mistake, he gets angry and heads for the door.

"Where are you going?" I plead. "You're drunk. Please, don't go out."

But he turns and hits me across the face.

It's the first time I feel like there's water, not blood, that runs through my veins. Like I'm watching myself from behind me. I don't want any of this. Who is this man?

"What is wrong with you? You hit me! Come inside! Please?" I say "please" because I believe it will snap him back to reality. Somehow he listens and I get him into bed. Petey stays under the table all night.

*I lie next to you,
an Apollo statue,
imagining a head,
at least limbs for
myself.*

The next morning we are largely silent. Then finally I say, "You hit me last night. Do you remember? You hit me."

108

Nothing.

The landlady is furious that Ishan bit her son's ear.

He stops drinking cold turkey.

Jim brings weed over one night, perhaps to help Ishan stay sober, perhaps because he's heard Ishan talking about how much he enjoyed it in India and how it helps mellow him out. Perhaps Ishan asked him to get him some. Ishan had stopped smoking years earlier, after his overdose, when I asked him to. Now, seven years later, he picks it up again. And decides to quit his job.

"I'll get another one."

It's the great recession. There are no jobs. Ishan goes on unemployment. One month. Two. Three. Five. Nine months before he gets a break. But in the meantime, he grows his hair long. Packs on twenty or more pounds. Completely gives up taking Petey for walks. He doesn't give up—he just says he isn't going to do that anymore. Picks up the guitar. Reads about bongs and vaporizers, researches growing weed.

I carry on, trying to complete an MFA while both of us get by on his unemployment and my tiny stipend, and each day I come home to this figure I don't recognize glued to the couch and computer. I wonder sometimes if he resents that I am completing my MFA in poetry, something we both loved, whereas he had to leave his job in New Jersey and move to Massachusetts in order for me to pursue this degree.

One day, he throws a shoe in my direction, but it doesn't hit me. Another time he kicks the chair I am sitting on. When he yells, I feel I can hear him before he opens his mouth. I'm afraid he will either throw something or hit me to release the tension. When you're afraid, you only become more afraid instead of seeing a way to step out to save yourself, or act. I say nothing. If I do, it makes things worse. Makes him more tense. He takes his frustration out on the dog and kicks him in the ribs. I wrap myself around Petey and we are both scared. *Fuck you, Ishan! I hate you*, I say in silence.

In my head, my own voice sounds like his. I do all my speaking in my head. On the outside, I say nothing because the moment I try, I will start to cry and he will get angry and yell at me to stop crying. Then the storm will pass and he will be sorry and I will feel guilty and sorry, too. I want to help him, but I don't know how.

19

After finding jobs again, Ishan, Petey, and I drive up to Acadia National Park in Maine to camp out. Ishan starts helping me take care of Petey again. But sometimes I catch him looking at the dog resentfully.

We climb Cadillac Mountain one day and it becomes obvious that Petey is hurting. His hip has been bothering him off and on for the past year. He stops a few times and will not budge.

Ishan explodes. He tosses the leash down and lets Petey go. "Fuck this dog! Motherfucker! I'm leaving him here. Stupid fucking dog! What good is he? I can't hike like this!"

Petey moves a few trees away; he's hiding and won't come. I'm worried he'll run away and we'll lose him on the mountain.

"Fuck off!" I yell back. "You can leave if you want to. I'm not leaving without Petey."

I have finally told him off. Calmly, I call Petey, telling myself he will listen to me. I wait for him to come, then grab his leash. He and I start going down slowly, our hearts in our mouths. Ishan is waiting for us; when we reach him, we start walking together again. A French couple catches up to us. Maybe they have heard us yelling, maybe not. But for the remainder of the walk, they walk at our pace and we talk a lot. I am surprised how good Ishan and I have gotten at switching to this nothing-happened kind of tone.

Later that week we catch the sunset on the other side of the island and get lobster at a shack there before going to check into a motel. We walk inside the restaurant and pick the lobsters they will cook for us. After we sit down, Ishan starts complaining.

"Man, Ani, you don't think! You know how expensive that's gonna be? Did we have to get lobsters? Did we? This place smells like shit. I'm out of here. Cancel the fucking order. I don't want it."

"But she's already making them," I say, my stomach in knots.

"I don't fucking care. I'm in the car. I don't want mine. You can do whatever the fuck you want."

And he gets up and leaves.

I don't know what to do. I wait and pay and get the lobsters to go, holding back tears.

What a fucking waste of perfectly good money and food. You fucking asshole, what is wrong with you!

I get in the car and he peels out of the parking lot. Petey seems to diminish in the backseat.

"I'm done. We're done, Ani. I'm not happy. We're not happy. Look at you. You're so scared. This is no way to be. You can't love someone you're scared of."

He chucks his cell phone out the window. What kind of person throws his phone out the window on a highway?

Later that night, someone calls me and says he found a phone on the side of the road and he's pretty sure it belongs to someone I know.

I will save this message from Michael in Bar Harbor for years. It's the first time in a long while that I hear a male voice and feel curious about it.

Inside the motel room, we eat one of the lobsters with our fingers. We have no utensils, and feed most of the rest to Petey. Ishan apologizes. We make up. We sleep holding each other but something is different now. I don't want to be with him anymore. I just don't know how to get out.

A month later, Ishan is granted U.S. citizenship. It has taken so long to get here. All the paperwork and interviews we have been through over several years and in three different countries: Thailand, India, and now the U.S. But I feel strangely numb. I notice nothing more than how the light enters the large windows illuminating the American flag. In a room filled with people and all their families, each one more enthusiastic and proud than the next—emotions I know well from when my own family was naturalized ten years earlier—I feel unsettled. I don't remember how we decide to celebrate, whether we get takeout from our favorite Chinese restaurant, whether we have dinner with our landlords, whether we stay home and cook. And I keep asking myself a question: How does such a big room full of tall windows feel so dark and constricting? At a time when so many experience something of a rebirth, all I can see is the end of my marriage. I don't ask Ishan if he feels the same. He looks happy, though he could look happier. And anyway, communicating with him has been going rapidly from bad to worse. I fear him more than I want to free myself. More than I dare to let us both go in peace.

Weeks after getting his citizenship, Ishan loses his job again. He gives up his guitar lessons and starts to smoke weed every day. There's something wrong. Why can't he hold on to a job? Then one day I am driving and I don't pass a car on the highway when Ishan tells me to, and he loses it. He kicks the windshield with his foot and cracks the glass. Later, I call the car insurance company, my heart pounding as I lie and say that I found my car in the supermarket parking lot with a crack on the windshield glass, and all I can think about is *I could be the cracked glass if I leave now.*

That fall, he discovers a winter hiking series that takes people up in the White Mountains between October and November. He is unemployed, but we have savings, so I encourage him to do it. Every weekend, he wakes up at four in the morning, leaves at five, drives three hours, hikes for seven or more, eats dinner with the group, then drives another three hours home. I don't know how he manages it physically. He never misses a class. He comes back feeling great, talks about mountains being magical, about how much he likes himself there, loves feeling his body tired, exhausted. His mind doesn't race with as many thoughts as it often does. As the weeks wear on, he goes on longer and longer hikes. Some mornings he wakes up and runs first. He starts running ten or more miles each time.

On Thanksgiving morning, still in bed, he tells me in a calm, almost wise tone, "I have to leave, Ani. I can't do this anymore."

"What do you mean?"

"We're done, Ani. We're not happy. I can't do this to you anymore. You will be fine, Ani. You're strong. I know this. You will be better off without a fucker like me. But I know I have to go. I'm sorry. I have to do this."

I cry. I understand he means it this time. It is over. His voice has the clarity of the morning after a monsoon rain. Nature has turned another page. The world has dropped or peeled off or washed away all around me. Or is it all the words we'd built this story out of? The language that had brought us together feels like a bandage now, soaked wet, falling off. I feel the most bare I have ever been. Completely lost. I also feel strangely held by something without language, a sense of relief that I don't have to leave or worry he would hurt me if I tried.

We have to go to my parents' for Thanksgiving that afternoon. We do one of those things we have perfected: we put on our happy faces and go. Nobody notices anything.

Back home, I cry all night. He kisses my forehead and says I will be fine. That I am strong. I will be better off than he will. He has to figure things out. Why he's like this. Find a job, etc. Is it okay if he stays here until then? Where else will he go?

He holds me and the quiet night holds us in a way that feels continuous, long into the future. It seems to hold our individual solitudes, our shared joys, all the sorrows we will ever experience, whether together or apart, and everything else in between. Entirely.

20

At first, I tell no one. I am too anxious to try to explain over the phone to long-distance friends that my marriage is over. Although I'm close to some colleagues at my new job, I can't bring myself to articulate to them what's going on in my life.

And then I hear something of a song. I decide to visit my cousins in Los Angeles and afterward, find myself on the plane home sitting next to an older woman. She asks if I'm married and notices my hesitation. I feel as though we've both just watched the same movie, only at different times; she tells me about her divorce many years before, and I find I can't keep anything from her. As my marriage unravels, I will sit in her Cambridge kitchen more than once. On one visit, she gives me a pepper shaker that her mother-in-law, Eva Zeisel, herself an immigrant from Hungary, has designed: a black bird, mouth and neck turned toward the sky, maybe singing, maybe anticipating being fed.

I don't tell my mother until six months later, when my father is away on research in Europe. He won't hear about it for another month. I visit my mother, give her a letter I have written, and say, "Please read this and then we'll talk." In the letter, I don't mention all the reasons the marriage is over. I explain to her that Ishan and I have made the decision together and we both think it is best for us. All she says is, "How is it possible?" and her favorite line, *Ç'të bën fëmija, nuk ta bën as Perëndia!* (What your children do to you, God himself would never dare!)

It's not that she's relieved I'm finally going to divorce the man she didn't like in the first place. And it's not that she wants me to stay with someone I am unhappy with. She's just calling it—all along it was my fault to find myself in this position. If I hadn't married Ishan, I wouldn't be divorcing him. What I did to her by marrying someone she didn't approve of was a mistake. She doesn't have to say any of this. I know it's what she means.

OUT OF THE LAYERS

21

THERE'S A FATHER I sometimes wish I had. He picks me up at school high-fiving me just as I run out the door into the schoolyard.

"How was it?" he asks. "How'd you do in the exam?"

"I nailed it!" I say, all joy and pride.

"Didn't I tell you?" my father says. "If you put in the work, you can do anything."

We walk the schoolyard together and all the boys—who'd later become men, who'd later ambush and stalk me—watch us, admiring how well I get along with my dad. I'm not afraid of them. They just wish they could be like my dad one day. When the time comes for them to ask someone out, they are no longer patrolling the streets. Instead, when their path crosses that of someone they're curious about, they know how to speak—they are all language, no touch. There is no need for them to grab girls by the wrists against their will because the boys simply open their mouths and say hello and the girls speak back to them if they want to. *Hello.*

But the boys who became men who ambushed, assaulted, and raped me and others will never know what it's like for a girl, or woman, to want to go out with them of her own free will. I have no forgiveness for them. I will not redeem them through writing. They can stay ingrained there in the 1990s streets of Tiranë, Albania, thinned-out smoky black shadows begging to know color.

The father I wish I had and I walk the school yard together, then cross the gate. The whole walk home he asks my opinion about things we pass on the street. This father is a friend of my mind.

The father I wish I had greets me after a long vacation away, opening his arms wide as a flag, waiting for me to hug him first.

This father reminds me of the father who took me to Theth National Park where the famous Accursed Mountains—the Albanian Alps—stretch out for more than forty miles and across the countries of Albania, Kosova, and Montenegro.

The winter I am seven, I get bronchitis, and the doctor advises my parents to take me to the Alps for a change of climate. My mother has to stay home with my brother, who is only two at the time. My father lets me play outside and even plays ball with me in a wide green meadow. We are shielded by mountains, tall

I have no memory of it.
I believe a river caught
    up with us
when we curved the
    foot of the mountain.
Men and women got off
    the bus to drink.

My father cupped his hands
and I gulped mouthfuls.

Snow patches led the way to
    the cool
black smoke of the woods.
    Over our heads
eagles played tag with the
    white sun.

and gray like tsunami waves that will never break. At dusk, he talks to friends he has made while sitting on the porch of the mountain villa where we're staying, and I can hang out and listen, although the moths collecting near the porch lamp have my undivided attention, green lacewings that take my breath away.

One evening, my father catches fireflies and uses the spit from his mouth to affix one to my forehead. This makes me feel briefly beautiful, with a light of my own. When I worry that a firefly had to die for me to feel this way, my

The way we changed the valley entering it like winter shadows.

father later assures me that no fireflies were harmed during these games. "Once the spit dries out," he explains, "they fly right off again."

During the day, my father and I go for walks and crunch dead cicadas in the grass, their bodies hollow shells like hard, tawny cellophane.

Where has the flesh gone?

My father doesn't know.

Cicadas can live underground for two to seventeen years before they emerge as nymphs, then shed their skins to begin their adult lives. Very rarely, it takes even longer, as with the strong little bug that Henry David Thoreau writes about at the end of *Walden*, "which came out of the dry leaf of an old table of apple-tree wood . . . from an egg deposited in the living tree many years earlier still."

*I never dream of it
but I remember being watched
as I stood at the edge of water
stirring images with my foot.*

22

The father I do have becomes the father I learn to avoid like all other men when I become a teenager. He slaps my butt, in passing, and early on in life, I learn to avoid being on the same path as him. I learn to be embarrassed of my own father. I learn to be on guard with men.

Many years later, at one of my readings, the father I wish I had stands at the end of the room and claps harder than anyone, telling them all that I'm his daughter. Some people mistake him for mad because he's too enthusiastic and won't shut up, but if they take time to listen, they hear him say: "That's my daughter. Right there stands my daughter. But I didn't make her. She birthed herself." And from the way his eyes and voice soften when he says that, they know he means what he says.

My father slaps my butt in the typical way adult men do, *in jest*, as so many men have done across cultures and time. The PE coach does it, when I am in seventh or eighth grade, and I often lie and say I am sick and sit by the school wall to avoid running past him. I see boys walking on the boulevards lifting their own sisters' skirts up for sport. It is fun for the boys. It is humiliating for the girls, who have no choice but to put up with it. Decades later, my brother tells me the boys of my neighborhood had heard that a girl was raped. "They'd sneer, pointing at her when she walked by," my brother recalls. He'd been just eleven years old, witnessing the sneering and pointing, absorbing the language.

Children learn misogyny when guests visit the family on special occasions and toast the long life of the son in the house, whether or not a family also has daughters. Daughters. Sisters. What were they? The lesser sex. In Albanian, the word for "mother," the root of which is almost the same across Indo-European languages, is attached to the word for "sister." *Moter* means *sister* in Albanian. Albanian is the only language I am aware of where such a phenomenon occurs, and here as elsewhere, language reveals more than we may be ready to admit. In Albania, a daughter takes on the role of mother for her siblings because her own mother has a duty to maintain the household, to clean and cook and serve her husband and his family. It falls on the daughter to provide emotional support to the siblings when her own mother can't.

My father doesn't know, doesn't realize that he has made me uncomfortable. I never tell him. Like other men around him at the time, in that place, he doesn't know what boundaries are needed. He has two sisters. One of them, fifteen years older, was his math teacher at school, whereas the other one is much younger than him. Neither of them are around enough to mother him in the Albanian sense of the word.

In general, Albanian men see women as objects. Albania has never seen a civil rights movement or sexual revolution. Men's role models are other men in the Communist party or other historical male nationalistic figures who have fought against the 500-year Ottoman oppression. In fact, because my father was raised with sisters and Christian parents in southeast Albania, and because he is a man of letters, I want to imagine that he is more understanding and self-reflective regarding women compared to typical men of his time. But the truth is, he is my good friend throughout my childhood, and rarely my friend when I am a teenager and young adult. How can you be friends with someone you're constantly embarrassed of or feel unseen by? I keep my distance for many years in America, too, for other reasons.

When I think of my father, I think of the man who comes home after work and, when I ask, "Dad, what did you bring me?" replies, "I brought you Dad!" It is a sweet joke, and I forgive him for coming home empty-handed. The truth is, I don't know that my family lives paycheck to paycheck. But I can't wait for the times when he brings me books from the library or bookstores in town. My father brings me the Albanian myths and legends and all the Greek ones. *The Odyssey. The Iliad.* All the Aeschylus tragedies, which I have read cover to cover several times. My imagination runs wild with all the gods and goddesses, all the humans who are sometimes smarter, and often have a stronger will than the gods.

23

My gynecologist has recommended that I see a sex counselor. She has already called and told this woman about me. So I go.

Jean's basement office is furnished with a beige leather couch, a black leather couch, a black leather chair, orchids, and other potted plants.

"That's for my husband's patients," she explains, indicating the black leather couch. "We both practice from this office."

Across the room is a desk where hot water waits in a bubbling kettle for coffee or tea. I choose coffee and sit on the beige couch. I notice a box of tissues on a lamp stand near me and small ceramic pieces of what look like fertility goddesses. It is a comfortable, quiet room. No windows.

"How can I help you today?" she asks. It's a question I will hear many times on future visits whenever I go quiet. She looks straight at me when she says it. She is well defined—that is what I notice first. Defined. Present. Real. Complex. Part mother. Part oracle. Part old friend. Part sexual. It is in the way she sits, directly across from me on the leather chair, as though she has come to seek advice from me. I can feel how comfortable she is in her skin.

Jean will become someone who teaches me to listen to language. I see her as a translator, a fellow linguistic traveler. She engages in deep listening the way I do when I translate poetry, listening not just for the words on the page, but also for the author's intent. I know she listens to my words because she remembers details I have shared. But she is most helpful when she listens for what I have not said. She helps me realize why or how one thing in my life connects to another. I have learned to ask my authors questions when I want them to realize that a word may need to change to capture more clearly what they've wanted to say. I have also learned from translators of my own work the importance, or irrelevance, of a word or description in the larger picture of the text as a whole.

"How can I help you?" Jean asks again, with the same direct gaze I'll soon learn will always make me talk. Her gaze doesn't have the piercing, hungry look I grew up with in Albania. Neither is it the judging kind. It feels like she can actually see me.

I think of my brother, who is now a psychologist. Sometimes I wonder how he—who, at five years old, told ten funny stories in a minute—grew up to be such a serious, responsible adult.

One day I ask him if we can talk about his work. "Do you think you rely on language more than people give you credit for?" I want to know. "What does it take for you to get to this point, to be something of a linguistic traveler? Have you ever thought of yourself this way?"

"It takes truly attuning to the client's inner and outer process," he answers. "To listen with the intent of understanding, not so much responding, and to always pay attention to themes instead of words."

I love this. He's five years younger than I am, and conversations like this between us are rare, but when they happen, my heart expands. I feel so proud of him.

"Themes instead of words! That's exactly it. But how do you become good at identifying themes?"

"Practice, and lots of training," he says after a pause. "And a good supervisor."

My brother is a private person. I would love to be closer to him, but I understand how much he carries from all the lives of the people he counsels. So much more space is required for him to feel safe within the life he has built with his family.

"I'm divorcing," I finally tell Jean. "My husband and I have never had sex."

While there are so many ways in which it's clear that my life with Ishan is toxic and I would be better off without him, I still long for the side of him I fell in love with—the man who reads my moods, who makes me laugh when I'm stuck or feeling down, who brings me breakfast and other small joys, who shares something he's fallen in love with and includes me in that discovery, who rubs my shoulders and teases me in Albanian. I'm not ready to let *us* go. A few nights ago, maybe because we both know it's over and we can taste a new freedom, he turned me on the way he had done years ago in that car in Thailand, fingering me as we were kissing, both in tears. What if we could finally have sex, I thought, with him inside me?

Jean wants to make sure I understand there are numerous definitions of sex, and I'm surprised I haven't thought that what Ishan and I have been doing is a type of sex.

"But you haven't had PVI," she says.

"What's that?" I ask.

"Penis-vagina intercourse."

"No. That we haven't."

"Did you and Ishan have other partners before you got married?"

I tell her no. And then I tell her about Ben, my neighbor when my family first moved to South Lancaster, a painter, dreamy with his medium-length ponytail, almond-shaped eyes, raised cheekbones and dimples. "He was my first kiss, later, when I moved to Boston. At twenty-three. First time I touched a penis." I hear myself tell Jean it was huge. "I probably said to Ben he'd kill me with that." We laugh, and I remember how much Ben and I had laughed, too. "Then he moved away to St. Croix and I to Thailand."

"What about in Albania?" Jean asks. "Did you have boyfriends there?"

My palms tingle and start to sweat. How do I tell her everything? How do I construct a story out of silence?

24

Initially, I seek Jean out because I think I can fix my marriage with confirmation that I have vaginismus, a gynecologic condition that describes pelvic floor muscle tightness and the involuntary tensing of the vagina when the insertion of an object such as a Pap test speculum, tampon, or penis is attempted. If we could just have sex, I think, maybe Ishan won't leave me; maybe we will learn a new way to be and know one another again. I want the diagnosis because I believe it will make me feel better about myself—if I have a treatable condition, that will remove the possibility that this is something I created myself.

But as Jean and I soon learn, I don't have vaginismus. At the gynecologist, I have my first real Pap test since Thailand. It is painful, but the doctor talks me through it, and her assistant stands right next to me holding my hand. I sense that they both know I can do this, that it will be okay. I cry. Not from any pain. I am relieved that I am finally going through it.

Ishan moves out. I begin reading Thich Nhat Hanh, *The Hite Report*, *Our Bodies, Ourselves*. I start CrossFit. I lose weight. Gain muscle. I have a crush on one of the coaches. I do nothing about it; everyone has a crush on him. I tell Jean about him.

One hot summer night, I spot a neighbor out walking his dog. He is shirtless, and greets me when he sees me walking Petey. I can tell he knows his bare upper body makes me uneasy. Petey sniffs around as though this time he is surely on to something. Another car passes to remind me that, in this episode, nothing happens. The shirtless man on that moonless night, beer belly hanging out, becomes the moon. I have no use for him. Deep down I wish he would burn through the canvas of this night. May his wife be watching open-mouthed from the window and not know what to do or how to call him back. Yes, I tell myself, I can wish and curse if I want to—I am mad with longing and it's been a long lacking season.

"Have you tried tampons?" Jean asks.

I tell her no. "Everything hurts," I say. "I can't insert anything in there. It feels like a sharp knife is trying to pierce me."

"Have you heard of Raquel Perlis?" she says. "She has helped so many women overcome pelvic dysfunction through physical therapy. Even people with vaginismus, although we both know you don't have that."

I want to believe her.

I call Raquel Perlis's office several times to try to get an appointment. It is impossible. She is booked several months in advance. But I realize there are more women going through this. I read about it online. There are success stories. There is a Women's Therapy Center in New York where for $10,000 you can go and stay for a few weeks and they guarantee your cure of vaginismus or other pelvic dysfunctions. Other websites list costs from $500 to more than $5,000. My gynecologist suggests I buy dilators. I tell Jean I am going to take this advice.

"Try a tampon first," she suggests.

Two weeks after Ishan moves out, I try it. I sit on my bed and think about the twenty-inch box at the gym that I could not jump onto when I first joined. At first, I can only jump onto the twelve-inch box. Then fourteen, then sixteen, then one day, I reach eighteen inches easily and the coach says, "Go for the twenty, Ani, you got this." "Oh yeah, totally," adds a teenager, who is my partner on that day, and maybe it's because both of them are saying it, maybe it's the fact that I've been doing this for a while now, but I have gotten stronger. I step back. "I fucking got this!" I tell myself, I jump, and damn! I land on the twenty-inch box like it's nothing. I put another inch plate on top and jump that, too. Then another, and another. I manage twenty-five inches and it's like my mind has expanded: I can envision doing something, then I do it.

Conquer fear, I tell myself now. I allow myself no other option. I use first one finger and then another, breathing and feeling myself relax and open, continuing to breathe as I first let the tampon touch me and then keep pushing it gently in. I notice that breathing is key and it helps me relax. The deeper I breathe, the longer I exhale and the softer and more pliant everything becomes. I tell myself the tampon is just something that will go in temporarily. It will come out again. I have tested the string earlier trying to pull hard on it to see if it might detach. I have dipped it in a cup of water to see how much bigger it will get. I have taken the time to understand how it works before I allow one to work inside me. I have looked at illustrations of the anatomy of a vagina. Jean has shown me an adorable velvety sponge-made vagina whose parts she named. It was a deep raspberry color, like something belonging to a wizard, I thought. I know its depth, the way I mentally know a route I have seen on Google maps. I have gone to the gynecologist, who has assured me there is nothing wrong with my anatomy.

I am able to insert one, but forget to push on the small part of the applicator before pulling the other part out. It is wrongly inserted and I have to discard it and try again. Once I get one in, it becomes increasingly easier to use them even in the gym, and in a pool, and then I never look back.

25

There I am, two weeks after Ishan has moved out. It's as though I can't even try when he is around. I have to be free of him before I can listen to my own body. When he's around, he is all that is around. There is no room for me. The space between us is ruled by too much fear and need. These, too, have now become small, final deaths.

My body knew what it wanted and what it didn't before I knew. My body and I were strangers to each other. I was not honest with myself or with Ishan. I think back to when we first met face to face—was I really attracted to him? I thought he looked beautiful and we were in love. Before we met, when he'd sent me pictures of himself, the streets and trees of his hometown, the people in his village, his dogs, his whole world, I remember loving that world but having a sinking feeling. How would or could I fit into his world? Could he fit in mine? Deep down I could hear the answer, but I had gotten very good at ignoring it. He said he loved me. I wanted a relationship—I was going to get one. Distance didn't matter. Cultural differences be damned. But deep down, I was deeply concerned. What if he couldn't control his use of weed, alcohol? But dating in Asia is neon-lit. In India and Thailand, Ishan and I walked through night markets, the euphoria of waterside restaurants and vibrant streets welcoming us. We had no financial worries. Marriage felt like the easiest thing to do. We were actors in a film where the ending is already presaged. The soundtrack—folk music in a language you don't understand but it draws you right in. The kind of movie that never tells you what happens after the wedding is over.

The truth is, I don't desire him. I don't even know what desire feels like. I felt something like this with Ishan the first few weeks we were together, but mostly, when he brushes past me in the kitchen, I don't feel a sudden stir, a headrush. I don't buy lingerie just to see what it will feel like to hide and reveal my body, what I want both for my own pleasure and what that feels like in front of someone. I don't feel wanted or desired and I don't know then that I would have enjoyed that. I know that I both love him and do not trust him. I know I fear him. How can you desire someone you fear? How can you desire someone you keep secrets from?

Jean often tells me "there are no rules" when I ask her if this or that action of mine is "normal." Perhaps not everyone needs to feel wanted in their relationship.

It's around this time that my divorce papers are being finalized. I am going through them with my lawyer and there is something in the separation agreement that bothers me: the word *disputes*. It is an inaccurate representation of why Ishan and I are divorcing, I tell my lawyer. I understand that it's a common legal word, and that the judge will skim through it, but to me, for my marriage and my divorce, the word does not fit. What I want, what feels true on the page, is *irreconcilable differences*.

Each morning, when my landlord starts the engine of his truck and prepares to leave for work, his black lab has a fit, running up and down their living room like an inmate in solitary confinement, barking and barking until the truck turns the corner and you can no longer hear its roar. I know the dog is not barking because he's talking to the human. By then, he is conditioned: the engine rumble is equal to my owner's leaving, my bark time.

Isn't it like this with a drawn-out marriage? She makes dinner. Sweeps the floors. Irons his favorite shirts and folds them neatly inside his suitcase whenever he goes on business trips. They get past the need for each other. They do their shopping together. She hates Christmas shopping the most because he can never make up his mind. It is her fault if she doesn't help him pick something out, and her fault if she does and doesn't convince him to let it go if it is too expensive. It always seems to hurt more to see him unhappy. She keeps spinning in this wheel.

Whatever she does, it isn't because she has to own something that matters. She already believes she has that. By then, they have carved their bodies so deep into that ancient tree, the tree we plant and tend when we're young in love, each branch a promise we make to one another. The branches grow more tangled with every promise that can't be kept. But how can anyone promise a fixed thing when the future changes constantly as we approach it?

How could we still make promises toward a future when our present had become stale and unfulfilling? Maybe we weren't that ambitious. Maybe we took each other for granted. Maybe we were both hopeless. Maybe neither of us had any idea what we were doing. I'm talking about that tree, the one we couldn't escape from. Or *I* couldn't. What I did was rest there, still, like the animal that gives up the fight when the snake is coiled tight around her body. I think you could say I even held my breath. I coiled myself up with my own beliefs in a reality I felt comfortable imagining I lived in. I had married the man I loved—that seemed to be a paramount goal. Patiently and intently husking my identity like it were an ear of corn. There was nothing in this picture about who I was or what I wanted for myself. I had accepted the ending before I'd allowed myself room to think that I could fight, that I could get out if I wanted to, that I could forge a different path. That I could still grow independent from the love of another.

No. I never want to be there again. Immolating myself for the sake of love.

PART TWO

ALL THE LANGUAGES A GIRL CARRIES

26

THE ALBANIAN LEGEND of Rozafa originates from the town of Shkodër, just north of Tiranë, where I grew up. Shkodër shares a border with Montenegro through Lake Shkodër, the largest lake in the Balkans. The Castle of Rozafa stands on a hill overlooking the meeting of two rivers: Buna from the northwest and Drin from the southeast. The castle is more than 2,500 years old, with its first stones said to have been laid when the Illyrian tribes of Labeats and Ardians lived in the land.

According to legend, a thick fog falls over the Buna River, covering it for three days and three nights. After three days and three nights, the fog lifts and the wind sends it over Valdanuz hill, where three brothers from the Labeats tribe work at building a castle to protect their people from others, as tribes often did in those days. Through it, the Labeats tribe founded and protected the city that would later become known as Shkodër. But the walls they build during the day inexplicably come down at night, all their hard work going to waste.

When an old wise man passes by one morning, the brothers

stop him to ask his advice on how to keep the castle walls from being destroyed every night. Hesitating at first, the old man asks each of them if they are married.

"Give your word of honor to each other," he says, "that you will not tell your wives when you go home today what I'm about to tell you."

Then he tells them that for the walls to stand, they must sacrifice the wife who brings them lunch the next day. She must be buried alive in the foundations of the castle for the castle to stand strong and last. The brothers promise one another that they will not say a word to their wives at home about this. However, the oldest brother tells his wife, advising her to come up with an excuse not to bring the men lunch the next day. So does the second brother. Only the youngest brother keeps his word and says nothing to his wife.

The next day, the mother of the three brothers asks her eldest daughter-in-law if she can take lunch to the men. The eldest says she can't because she isn't feeling well. The mother asks the second daughter-in-law, who in turn also says she can't, because she needs to visit her own family. So the mother turns to the youngest daughter-in-law, who is ready to go, only she is worried her newborn son will be left at home crying and needing to be nursed. The other two daughters-in-law quickly offer to take care of him, and without further discussion, the youngest one sets forth to take lunch to the brothers.

When her husband sees her coming up the hill carrying a pot of wine on her left shoulder and a tray of bread under her right arm, he throws down his hammer and starts cursing the stones.

"Why do you curse the stones, love?" Rozafa asks him.

"Cursed is the day you were born," the eldest brother responds. "We've agreed to bury you alive in the foundations of the castle so that the castle walls will last."

"May you prosper," she replies, "but I have one request: When you bury me, leave my right eye exposed, my right breast, my right arm, and my right leg, too. Because my son is still so little. When he starts to cry, I will watch him with my eye, I will caress him with my hand, rock his cradle with my foot, and feed him with my breast."

This part has always terrified and fascinated me, imagining how a human being could live, or die for that matter, with her body half buried and half exposed to the forces of nature. And what became of her middle? As a child, I wondered what happened to her . . . hole, down there. Was half of it left exposed and if so, why? Decades later, as an adult, I will learn about the last ancient goddess, Sheela-na-gig, who is not a Rozafa at all, not selfless or walled-in, who will answer this for me.

"May my breast turn to stone," Rozafa says, "and may the castle stand strong. May my son grow to be brave, become king, and reign for a long time."

They bury her as she requested. The castle walls are built tall and last for many centuries, to this day. They say the stones at the feet of the castle's walls are moist, covered in moss, and that when it rains, the white liquid that spills from them is Rozafa's milk still flowing to nurse her son.

Albanian women love hard, from beyond the grave.

137

27

It is Meropi's faith that gets my family to the U.S., along with Ligor and his constant chanting, "Go to America, you must go to America." Meropi prays for us to win the green card lottery. Then, in 1995, it happens. My father wins the U.S. Diversity Visa lottery. He is ecstatic, a child at fifty-two. He comes home that day laughing, clapping his hands, jumping around. We have won the green card lottery! We will be going to America. America! Someplace far away, where everything works and anyone can get a job. I begin to dream about finally being able to walk freely on any street I want to. I dream of what it will feel like to finally look a man in the eyes. A man, or anybody really. It feels like I am saved. My life will start over. I don't think about my parents' lives, what it will mean for them at forty-eight and fifty-three to move to a country where they don't speak the language, with two teenagers in tow.

On July 4, 1996, at eighteen years old, I leave behind all that I know—my friends, my relatives, my grandmother, my town and its streets—and move to this huge country whose language I'm not yet fluent in. I weep for hours on the airplane. The first memory I have of arriving at Logan Airport in Boston is an officer trying to take my fingerprints at the checkpoint. My parents and

Put your finger here,
he says, *look over there*. Over there

stands my family, waiting, as if to see
me off.
He tries once more: *Put it down here,*
look over there. Doesn't he know
this has nothing to do with fear? There,

just like getting a shot, it's already over.
I check in and walk toward the crowd,
thinking music:
Put it down here, look over there.
Tá ta ta / tá; Tá ta ta / tá.

138

brother get through right away, but I'm stuck because the machine can't read my prints—my hands are too sweaty. The officer grows impatient. I can hear it in the way he says, "Put it down here, look over there," repeating the same line as though he's going to give me an injection I'm afraid to watch. He wipes my finger with a cotton cloth and the words *here* and *there* become a dance, a spell, the way they seesaw through the air.

When he finally gets my fingerprints, I walk toward my parents, Albania and America balanced on both sides, the seesaw coming to a stop, at least for now.

I didn't know then that I would continue to live on this lever, integrating *here* and *there*—Albania and the U.S., my identities as a poet and a writer, as a professor of creative writing and a high school ESL teacher, as a literary translator and a linguistic traveler—that one day, more than twenty-five years later, I would be walking toward my parents in a different way, giving back to them in words the kind of home they never conceived of finding here the morning we left Albania.

That afternoon, we step out of the Boston airport into a taxi beneath impossible skies open to the horizon. Highways so wide they seem endless. Cars race by, trees, streets, houses, squirrels. There are celebrations on the street and for a few long moments it feels like this country has come out to welcome us. We are settling in South Lancaster, a small town an hour west of Boston known for being the cradle of the Seventh-day Adventist faith. We know no one in America except for a distant relative in Worcester, so my parents chose

South Lancaster on the advice of American missionaries at our church in Albania.

As soon as we arrive, we are the new show in town. Everyone wants to get to know this family from Albania whose grandmother has recently become a beacon of faith for the Seventh-day Adventist church. They have written about and discussed Meropi all over SDA TV channels and magazines around the world. It is the early nineties, and the borders have just opened after the collapse of Communism, allowing missionaries from all religions to descend on Albania. Adventists don't know much about Meropi. But they are in awe when they discover that my grandmother has saved over five hundred dollars in tithes. For nearly fifty years, Meropi has kept this money, faithfully, month after month, hidden in a cookie tin under her bed. That may sound like nothing at all now, but to an Albanian in the early nineties, that money could buy a beautiful, spacious house.

Meropi is happy that we are living in a town full of other Adventists. In her isolated religious life, Adventists are angels. In truth, most of them seem to be selfless people who welcome us and find jobs for my parents, give us food, clothes, furniture, or invite us over for countless meals.

While I no longer feel like I'm being followed by so many men or watched for my family's political beliefs, the feeling of being judged continues for me here in America. Most of my friends and the people in our community don't consume meat, shellfish, or drink alcohol. While our lives in Albania were not exactly feasts of shrimp, lobsters, and wine, now I have to check myself if I go out for a meal with an SDA friend. Like my grand-mother, I like the SDA teachings as far as being able to pray to God directly rather than in the presence of a priest. But my atti-tude toward the SDA faith is increasingly that it feels like a reli-gion for the rich. Seventh-day Adventists own their own health food stores that sell a variety of meat alternatives and delicious, flavorful granola my new-immigrant family loves but can rarely afford. From sundown on Friday to sundown on Saturday, secular activities and work aren't allowed, not even grocery shopping, which has to be done ahead of sundown on Friday. Saturday's meals must be prepared ahead as well. Adventists hold the teachings of Ellen G. White—one of the co-founders of the SDA church who was said to have had the gift of prophecy—in such high regard that she is like a second Jesus. I have always been wary of humans who come between me and my God. For all of these reasons, I am now finding it hard to relate to many parts of the faith. And at some point in my twenties, it will no longer make sense to me to wait a whole week to worship God on the Sabbath when I am mindful of God in every decision I make.

For now, though, I continue to keep the Sabbath and pay the tithe. I will continue to do so until I return from Thailand, but I already choose to eat out sometimes on a Saturday, or eat shrimp with some of my Adventist friends who are, like me, less strict about these things. I purchase things on Saturday if I forget to purchase them before sundown on Friday. I donate when I can where I see it's most needed instead of giving one tenth of every-thing I make to only one place. I decide that God has common sense, that restrictions and bargains are human customs.

I grew up under my grandmother's teachings from the Bible, and she did not grow up with Ellen G. White's prophecies. Neither my family, nor my grandmother, had access to those and other materials that people who are raised Adventists in free countries do. Meropi had heard about and admired Ellen a great deal. In fact, she told us many times that if we hadn't been struggling economically in Albania, she would have chosen a vegetarian life and encouraged my family to follow. But not having been raised with typical Adventist teachings all our lives made me and my family slightly more curious about what it means to live a Christian life rather than a specifically and strictly Adventist one. In truth, because my grandmother was curious about Adventism to begin with—the idea that we can approach God directly in prayer rather than through a priest—being an Adventist has always felt to me both like an opportunity and a challenge to keep an open mind.

28

When we move to America, I am eighteen and my brother is thirteen. Countless peers and adults at school ask us the same question.

"Where are you from?"

"Albania."

"Oh, is that in Russia?"

"No. You know Italy, Greece? It's right above Greece, east of Italy." I try to offer a semblance of familiarity, not realizing I am playing a part in relegating Albania even further to the margins.

No one asks me, "What did you love to do back home?" If they did, I would tell them about my brother's stories, how I loved to listen to him imitate the sound of hand grenades—*eeeeeeeaaah baauudoufff*—after movies we watched of Albanians fighting off Germans during World War II. How, afternoons when our parents were at work, I toasted bread layered with snow-white sugar sprinkled with olive oil for him. How we sat and watched *crtani film*—cartoons—from Yugoslav channels, biting into the sweetness and the translucent green of the oil, the toasted crust browning underneath it like the contours of an underwater city we have yet to see.

There is no ESL program at my brother's school. He learns English from scratch, all on his own. I can't even imagine what trauma that causes—sitting in silence not understanding what everyone around you is saying so many hours of the day, five days a week, week after week, month after month, until he begins to piece it together for himself.

How does it happen? How do I adopt the English language so quickly? Do I consciously reject my homeland? My identity? My non-identity? After all, I have not "survived" girlhood in Albania. I have avoided it. Does that absence mean I am forging a new identity? What kind of person seeks to find a new way of being in another language? Everything in English suddenly feels real and new again, alive. When I write my essays as a college student I feel a thrill at discovering that I mean what I write. For the first time in a long while, teachers ask me to say not just what I think, but explain why. I am given time with my

It's snowing in a way
   that reminds me
of people who rarely complain.

I imagine the oldest woman
   eating bread: silent,
half asleep, softly chewing
mngna, mngna, mngna.

thoughts. Now when poems come to me or I go after them, the same feeling follows—excitement at discovering concise ways to express thoughts and emotions that were foreign or lost to me until now. English makes me feel like I can think again.

I arrive at English the way I imagine someone must arrive on the night of prom. It is an entrance. The way a seventeen-year-old in the movies enters the ballroom and is not recognized at first—no one expects her to look this beautiful—but of course it's her, everyone can see, and the whole night belongs to her. But I am not in a movie. This is real. I see myself the moment I begin to write poems in English. Like film developed in a dark room, I am no longer in negative, but in full color.

So much of who we are is affected by the language we use, and the language everyone speaks in Albania is a language of secrets: "Don't talk about God outside," my grandma warns almost daily; "Watch out you don't mention this to Bela," my mom warns about my friend. A language of secrets and harassment. "Where do you think you're going?" "You're not going home today." "I'm not letting you go anywhere." "Shut up!" A language of political lies and manipulations and crimes. "Did you hear about Mehmet Shehu? [Shehu has spoken out against Enver Hoxha.] They killed him in the middle of the night." And on TV, Enver Hoxha says, "Albania is the luminous beacon of the world." "The Party does what the people

I am thankful for snow
and the black stillness of evergreens
the way they line up on the street
here in my New England.

want and the people do what the Party says." I am a child, but I can taste something bitter in this language. I don't want to eat that bowlful of dirt.

And yet, it is in Albania where I also fall in love with foreign languages. English first, from the age of eight to twelve, when my father signs me up to take private lessons twice a week. Then Italian—my neighbor is a great teacher who tutors me for a year. In high school, I major in Russian, a language that, in

I have made it mine, the way a young girl finds someone's lipstick and makes it hers.

the eyes of a corrupt Ministry of Education, is reserved for those whose parents aren't Communists, or can't afford to enroll their kids in English, the popular choice after the regime's collapse, or even Italian or German, next in line. Being thrown into this language I know nothing about and whose alphabet is so different from my own, my mind twists and bends to learn new verb tenses and conjugation forms for nouns and adjectives.

I don't know if or when I might write in Albanian again. I don't switch to English because I am renouncing my Albanian identity. I do it because I have no identity. English is the language in which I learn about poetry and other writers I admire. Thoreau's words, "If a man does not keep pace with his com-

It doesn't matter that it's half used
it matters that it's lipstick and she wears it
down to her chin.

panions, perhaps it is because he hears a different drummer," deeply reach me and unleash a voice and vision I had no idea belongs to me. I am writing. It's all about Albania. The journey into English. I let it come.

29

After arriving in the U.S., I do everything I can to improve my English as quickly as possible. I learn so much of it just by reading Emily Dickinson, whose use of language and ways of seeing what surrounds her are so new that I begin to memorize many of her opening lines. I try to perfect my accent daily, speaking in my head or to myself at night in bed, so that I will sound more like a native speaker. I think that if I can assimilate right away, I can leave behind the years of fear and anxiety I lived through in Albania. I want those years to be gone, forgotten, to never catch up with me. I wish for a magic comb, like the one in Grimm's fairy tales, that you can throw at anything chasing you and it transforms into a mountain made of a thousand sharp teeth. I think I can create that kind of distance between myself and Albania—I work so hard that I manage to jump into regular college classes after only a semester as an ESL student.

Becoming a college English major is what eventually builds my fluency in English. Atlantic Union College is a small liberal arts Seventh-day Adventist school. We attend chapel every Tuesday: an hour filled with announcements, prayer, testimony, and singing. Most of the time I don't even open my mouth. I like to hear hymns in church, but I resist the expectation to pray whenever everyone rises. Why would God be pleased, or listen, if I did all this? Why would God expect anything at all, much less rituals orchestrated in the particular order that humans have prescribed?

I am reading Dickinson in one of my classes:

> Some keep the Sabbath going to Church—
> I keep it staying at Home—
> With a Bobolink for a Chorister—
> And an Orchard for a Dome.

I immediately understand what I am. I have always felt God present in nature and often just present everywhere. I can easily close my eyes and pray in bed or anywhere else, and in nature, I feel a kinship and communion with both living and dying things. But in church, in the presence of many, closing our eyes at the same time, it feels like a performance. I am a Dickinsonian.

Shortly after starting classes at Atlantic Union College, I find work at the G. Eric Jones college library. The library's director, Margareta, takes me under her wing the moment we meet when she finds out I speak Italian, her husband's mother tongue. A foreigner herself, she moved to the U.S. from Sweden after falling in love with Alberto. Margareta is one of the first people who selflessly tries to help me and my parents from the moment she hears we are new immigrants in town.

My lover wants me
to teach him languages
so I sit with him and begin.

I will teach you *pollés glósses*
all the glósses that you *théleis*,
théleis like they say in Greek
when they want something,
tell me what you théleis
and I give, I say.

I begin working at the circulation desk. It isn't easy, as it forces me to speak to people, including the young men I have crushes on, whose books I check out. But it also forces me to use my English and interact with people rather than avoid them. It is English first and, later, writing, that will continuously push me to step out of my comfort zone.

After the circulation desk, I work in the interlibrary loan department; later, I'm asked to take care of the Special Collection Room where Dr. Ottilie Stafford, the most well read, prominent English professor of any Adventist university, has donated twentieth-century poetry books, a collection which the library will take great care to expand in her honor over many decades. Here, I discover voice through Marianne Moore, that a poem can read like a story through Elizabeth Bishop, come right off the page to slap or cradle you through Sharon Olds, that words are alive and spark against each other through Wallace Stevens, that line breaks fix a rhythm on the page through A. R. Ammons, that love can transcend distance through Rupert Brooke, that it's a woman's poetry that will pierce me deeper than a man's through Ai and Maya Angelou, that there's something I taste in e. e. cummings's poetry that brings more pleasure than W. B. Yeats's or W. H. Auden's, though I never tell Professor Stafford that.

Whenever new books arrive, I add them to the shelves where

You have to be *silenzioso* though when I speak
and listen *soltanto* to me,
that means you have to listen
very *attentamente*,
looking at my mouth,
my lips *specialmente*

and when I tell you, *amour*,
répète after *moi*,
you will repeat so *parfaitement*,
that I will say *bravó, bravó mon Dieu*,
I would even call you by such a
    name, I would,

they will be organized according to the Dewey decimal system.
I look through various publishers' catalogs and make decisions
as to which books we should add to the collection. That feels
important. As an English major in this new position, I have
some say in what can go into this room. When
I find Wallace Stevens's *Collected Poems*, I am   you, God of my words.
taken by the cover on which Stevens seems
to be standing in space, a constellation of snow flurries behind
him. I am struck by his imagination, how he can describe the
mind in the act of reading, how he can become a mind of winter,
capturing the process my own mind will go through. He is the
only poet I feel has real power over how a reader can think.

It's around this time that I meet my neighbor Ben, who, along
with his sister, is one of the first people to teach me how to drive.
Our parents are friends; Ben's parents have immigrated to the
U.S. from Germany and they, too, are Adventists. I have a crush
on Ben, but he has a girlfriend, so I never say anything. When I
enter grad school a few years later, after hearing that he is single
again, I write him a postcard asking if he'd like to go out sometime.

On our first date, we watch *The Lord of the Rings* at the movie
theater, and afterward, when he drops me off, he leans over to

kiss me. The car goes silent like a lake
filling up with snow; I slowly turn and   Then I would speak Albanian,
give him my cheek. I have dreamed of   and you'll say Shqip is the best
him, I think, the way a person dreams   language, *o zemër*,
of meeting someone they can kiss and   the most *bukur, bukur*
fall in love with—one of those dreams   beautiful, beautiful, and *voilà*,
that coil and coil, that becomes the
                                                                  it will color your thoughts red,
                                                                  redder, like that Russian blood,
                                                                  красный, прекрасный and last,

149

shell you retract into, when meeting the real person paralyzes you.

One day, after a creative writing class, partly forced by having procrastinated on keeping a daily journal and partly because there seems to be a fire inside me, I come home and sit outside on the fire escape stairs of our apartment and write poems. They're mostly four to six lines long, some longer. It is the first time I write poems in English and the first time I write like that for hours in one sitting. I feel as though my mind belongs to a greater mind. I read Lorna Dee Cervantes, ricocheting line after line from English to Spanish to English so effortlessly. I don't have her wisdom, but I try on her style.

the *culminación* of my teaching *será*
when I say shut up, *no repitas nunca más*,
just tell me, in what language
will you now describe my eyes?

Other days I go back to the Special Collection Room to read a page by Yeats or Bishop or one of their letters, or to just look, one more time, at a Rupert Brooke photo. I feel momentarily guilty that I am getting paid to work here, but I can't resist reading a few pages. I suppose people shouldn't hire poets to work in libraries! My mother always tells me, *Mos ja jep shpirtin punës* (Don't give your soul to your job). I have always taken those words to mean that it's important to find space within the work hours for joy to bloom, be it in the few minutes I could steal to read a page or two in that room or even now as a seasoned teacher, to stop lecturing and ask my students how they are on a given day, in that moment, to hear them for who they are rather than following the day's lesson plan to a tee.

Encountering poetry while building fluency in another tongue feels magical. The way that language works at figurative levels sparks my imagination. But mostly, how language finds me when it arrives in another tongue feels charged. In English, I begin to see possibilities of meaning that are new and original in my new target language. And in the process, I arrive at a new way of seeing what my past has meant to me—at least the parts I'm willing to remember.

CROSSING OVER

30

THE STATE OF THE ALBANIAN middle-class family under
Communism is the same as that of the Albanian lower-class
family. At least once a week, my father stands in line at 2:00
a.m. to buy a one-liter bottle of milk, which arrives sometime
before sunrise; the whole family is allowed half a dozen eggs,
half a kilogram of cheese, and one kilogram of meat per week,
rationed in such a way that every kilo of meat is comprised of
300 grams of bones, 200 grams of fat, and only 500 hundred
grams of actual meat. My parents' accounts are often emptied
before the next paycheck comes in. And yet, they make time for
family vacation every summer. When I ask my mother about
it now, she replies, "What vacation?!" and laughs with a little
unease, as someone does when trying to smooth over the rough
truths that just escaped her mouth. "I was mostly indoors cooking all day for the whole family, or your father's friends who
joined us sometimes."

It's true—those friends, or my aunts and uncles and their
children, join us for a few days at a time, sometimes for the

whole two weeks. It is fun to have cousins and friends around, and I hardly give a thought to what the adults are doing. For my brother and me, these vacations are what we look forward to, to go splashing on the beach with all the other children, to build another sand castle on the shore, to collect the next razor, scallop, or conch shell.

There are moments when I hear my mother yelling, and only after I grow up do I understand her frustration. The happiness and success of a vacation for the entire family fell on her—and the role of the Albanian woman under Communism is the same across the country. She works full-time outside of the house, does all the housework when she comes home, looks after the children, cooks, takes care of the in-laws if they live in the same house. This manifold job follows her on vacation. Remember Rozafa?

While I am someone who keeps everything inside, my mother lashes out. I can almost predict it. The house starts to sparkle; it builds up like irregular bursts of static frequency— "Damn! . . . another dish! . . . I'll scream if I want to, let them all hear!"—and then grows louder as if her mouth is a conch shell booming right into my ear. Sometimes I play outside in the dirt and I can hear other mothers, their frustrations issuing from open windows on the third floor, or the fourth, or the one on the bottom, to the right—little balloons that never lift off, but puncture and go flat as soon as they escape.

My father spends more time with his books than with his family. For over twenty years, he was a professor of Albanian literature and linguistics at the Academy of Sciences in Tiranë.

But speaking no English at fifty-three, and landing in a rural Massachusetts town of under eight thousand people, presents a problem when it comes to finding a job. Options are few.

See my dad those days, riding a bicycle to work and to evening ESL classes through sun, rain, snow. He works long days and I don't see him when he returns home at night. Some nights I see him lying on the floor, but not to pray like his mother used to. He lies flat on the hard floor because his back hurts. He works as a dishwasher. A prep cook. A security guard. On an assembly line for plastic molded parts. I am eighteen, nineteen, twenty, twenty-one, embarrassed of my dad's jobs, his old car and clothes. On special occasions or church days, he puts on a suit and I breathe easy again. I want my new American friends to see that my immigrant dad is as well off and independent as their own. I ignore the fact that both my parents did the most independent thing only a few can do: they left a way of life to start over from scratch somewhere else, no matter the sacrifices.

There are so many versions of my mother. My young mother wearing white with a headband in photographs from her college days. My mother, the officer in uniform. My mother, the poet who used to meet with another poet friend and take me along some afternoons when they would sit down and spread out pages and pages of typed poems on the floor and couches and talk and talk and I was bored out of my mind and couldn't wait to leave. My mother, the giving neighbor and sister—twenty-plus years in America and still she sends clothes and money to her family back home. The worried mother. The understanding, sometimes frustrated daughter-in-law. My mother, the she-does-everything-in-the-house wife. My mother, the immigrant. It's this mother I want you to see.

I have a photo of her before I was even an idea and a photo of me taken at the point when memories finally began to stick. I put the two together and snap a third photo—now we are conversing. This is the woman who crawled pregnant under freight trains to get to her job at a military unit an hour's drive away from home. She worked as a financial advisor there. I can't imagine what she must have thought of on those train tracks. Whenever I ask her about it, she says, "Ah, the dreams I dreamed of you," and I believe her. Perhaps, too, being the oldest of five daughters and the second child of eight, she may have wished for me to fulfill dreams she herself could not afford to realize.

She would arrive on those tracks even before dawn, crawling under the parked trains, the railway pebbles under her feet clacking like so many little skulls. I have no idea what a pregnant woman thinks about when she thinks of what she hasn't birthed yet. I imagine she weaves a million possible lives, affixing a million worries to each. Or maybe that's just my mother.

At forty-eight, with her fifty-three-year-old husband and two grown children, she moves all the way across the world to a different culture, to a land where she doesn't speak the language. She starts to push carts in a Shaw's supermarket parking lot. When I think of this, I realize why, when I need her the most as a young teenager in a new country, she isn't there. She is walking home crying from more thankless jobs she has taken on as an immigrant. Maybe because she is the newest hire, maybe because she doesn't speak any English then, she says she is the only one constantly being asked to go collect shopping carts from the parking lot and bring them in, rain or shine. In Albania, she'd published two collections of poetry. No one here cares about that; she doesn't have the fluency to tell them about it. When she vacuums another building where she works, a blonde Christian woman in her seventies who mans the front desk asks her, "How's your friend?" referring to the vacuum.

See my mother push those carts, see her cook for over 500 people in the college cafeteria where she is often simultaneously the cook, the cook-helper (on days when the student workers ask if they can leave early to study for an exam), the cashier, the kitchen cleaner. See her clean houses in several New England villages.

Sometimes I think I do not know this woman. She yells and huffs and puffs and writes poetry like eating bread. By that I mean she writes and writes and hardly ever revises. I love her for it! And then she shakes all of that off and I can almost hear her—she's like a tree whose branches are covered with tiny little bells, but to see this tree, you have to imagine it shuffling down the road, it's not rooted at all, and once it comes, it comes to stay where you stay. And if you want to stay in one place, she'll stay there with you. She'll grow roots for you. There's a light in her, so bright it grows from here all the way to those cold, starless nights in Albania under the freight trains. No wonder she could cross over. In my photo collage of us, the light seems to hold us both. I love that in these pictures, both our lips are parted. We have just told each other everything. We are about to say so much more.

While my mother puts her shoulder to the wheel and works more than one job, my father finds a seasonal job as a dishwasher at a country club. He gets the winters off, during which time he researches and writes about the journeys of Apostle Paul. He is convinced, my father, and after many years he is able to prove that Apostle Paul traveled to Albania and was solely responsible for bringing Christianity there in A.D. 50-60. Our dining room table becomes a fortress, constantly filled with library books. My father's English improves as a result, and in a span of eight years, he writes the most important book of his career, accompanied by a new biography of Apostle Paul. In twenty years, he publishes a third book on the topic, much better researched and documented. This book is well received in Albania and brings him further critical acclaim. The city of Durrës, the port city to which Apostle Paul traveled and from which he wrote several of his letters, recognizes the merits of my father's work and honors him. That's who he has always been: a scholar and a writer. He can't use these skills to make a living in the U.S., but he keeps feeding his passions and completes his books. My mother, too, continues to write, and publishes three more collections of poetry. Each one of them is that little strong beautiful bug coming out of the layers—and in that, I am both of my parents' daughter.

3 1

As immigrants, neither of my parents are ever offered full-time jobs. They remain locked at thirty-eight or thirty-nine hours a week, at minimum wage, which means they never get full-time benefits.

When I'm in college, one of my mother's jobs is at a book bindery in town. Her second job is to clean the three-story conference building of the Seventh-day Adventist Church, its offices, hallways, bathrooms, and dining areas, three hours a day and six on weekends. And although my father lives mostly in his head, seemingly aloof, he will often go with my mother to help her finish her second job in half the time.

Sometimes, I walk home from an evening class at the same time that my parents are walking home from work. But their work isn't over. We live in the English Department of Atlantic Union College where in exchange for looking after the building, we don't pay rent. It includes a third-story apartment, and when I hear that the couple living in it are graduating, I ask if I can apply to move in with my family.

Once we are accepted, we have rooms to ourselves for the first time in our lives. The apartment comes with a living room, a separate dining room, a kitchen, and a bathroom. A whole other wing of rooms serves as storage for the department. We use it as storage, too, and my brother makes his music room there with his drums, guitars, and his friends.

After all their day's work, my parents come home to work some more: they clean the six offices, five classrooms, five hallways, three bathrooms, common room, and kitchen. My brother and I sometimes help, all four of us at night, one person sweeping the floors in a classroom upstairs, another taking out trash from an office on the first floor, each of us doing something different at four different corners, the house lit in the middle of the woods, so if anyone looks at it from Main Street two hundred meters away, they can see us moving through those rooms like ballet dancers in a vintage music box.

The building is an old mansion built in 1883, all white on the outside, righteously gaining its pseudonym, the White House, with a wide front- and backyard surrounded by evergreen and pine trees, wood floors on the inside, wood on the walls and ceiling, tall antique leaded glass windows, professors' offices that look like so many private library rooms in a rich uncle's mansion. We love this house. In Albania, we had lived with my grandmother, all five of us, in 500 square feet for eighteen years. This is the only time we feel we have a home as a family, and we work in it, certainly my parents do, as if it is something more than our very own. The faculty will often praise my parents' work to me and to them. They tell us how much the place is flourishing since my family has moved in. My father plants flowers around the house: tulips, roses, bleeding hearts—my mother's favorite. My mother stitches up parts of a curtain or couch cushions in the common room, taking care that they look good again.

But even here, the brunt of the work falls on my mother's shoulders. She does all three of her jobs Monday to Friday and six hours on Sundays. My brother and I study. My father studies, too, in the winters. My brother and I are embarrassed of our parents' work and avoid them if they happen to be walking by in their work clothes when we are out with our friends. Classism starts at home.

At the schools where I teach now, I often stop to talk to the janitors and wish I hadn't been so embarrassed of my parents who did everything, without complaining, to secure a roof over my head, food on the table, clothes, and time to study. They did their jobs and did them well, even while battling depression. I was performing a role I picked up somewhere between watching *Beverly Hills, 90210*, *Dawson's Creek*, and other TV series and films made in America, one in which it mattered most to be and look cool. I worried those days whether I had enough mascara, mood rings, the right length jean shorts and white tank top, that my hair was finally long. Thinking about how I could have helped my parents juggle several jobs, house chores, and their own health was the last thing on my mind. My goal was to blend in as an American teenager. But the only reason there's any American in me is because of my parents.

Today, they live in a one-bedroom apartment in an affordable housing community for the elderly. My dad has a small plot in their community garden where he loves to grow vegetables, mint, basil, nettles, and some other things I can't name. My mother has arthritis in both her knees, which developed within a decade of moving to the U.S. When my mother was crawling under freight trains with me still in her belly, none of us knew she was then practicing how she'd cushion the way my brother and I landed in this country so that we could have dreams to follow.

32

When I'm in my thirties, I ask my father if he remembers the early nineties in Albania.

"Did I ever say anything to you or Mom about men stopping me on the street and harassing me? Did you know that this was going on for me and other girls on an almost daily basis?"

"No," he says, pausing to think before adding, "we would hear about young girls being kidnapped, but you never talked much about anything . . . And you didn't develop as fast as your other girlfriends."

"What do you mean?" I raise my voice, already angry, already uncomfortable, realizing my own father had been noticing my friends' bodies were changing, forgetting that of course he would. Wouldn't anyone?

"What do you mean? That it was okay for guys to harass girls once they looked more mature physically?"

"No, no," he laughs, nervous. "I just didn't think anything would happen to you because you didn't look—"

I don't want to hear him finish that sentence. I didn't look girly enough? I didn't have big enough breasts? I didn't wear skirts? I didn't have long hair?

"Did you see other girls on the street getting harassed, Dad? Did you ever intervene?"

"Only one time," he says. "I tried to stop them. It was raining one day and two guys seemed to be annoying a young girl." (Even he says *annoying* instead of *harassing*.) "I called at them from a distance. One of them turned to me holding his umbrella high in the air and threatened to hit me with it if I didn't mind my business. But I kept walking toward them and yelled at them to leave the girl alone so they ran away."

"What did the girl do?"

"She probably went home."

"Wow. You saved her. Did this stuff happen any other time?"

"No, nothing except that time. But we went off to work early, before anyone went to school. And we came back late. We didn't see any of this except when we would come to school to see you or to meet your teachers. Once, one of your teachers told me the situation was hopeless for the junior and senior year girls. As soon as they'd finish classes, or during recess, these unemployed young men were outside waiting by the school wall to hit on them, 'take them on a walk,' he would say."

"Did he say anything to you about me?"

"He said I was lucky that my daughter was still a freshman, but wait another two years and I would have hell to deal with. That's one of the main reasons why I applied for the green card lottery and why we left the country."

I was never aware back in 1996, when we left Albania, that my parents chose to leave their homeland partly to protect me. I had thought they left for economic and political reasons. If only I had been close enough with my dad to have confided how hard it was to be a girl all those years. If only he had thought it important enough to ask me. Instead, he wasn't there in the ways that I needed him. But when he realized he needed to move the family out of Albania, it was the one time that made all the difference.

Later, I will ask the same question of an old classmate I find online. He tells me he was too busy confronting the "scumbags of the neighborhood"—thieves and bullies—to understand how to protect his female friends. "I have to admit," he writes, "I followed you a couple of times on my bike after you finished school, in high school. I'm sorry! But that was our understanding back then of what you should do if you like someone! That's how you did things post-Communism. Who was there to show us what to say to a girl?"

It is the first time I learn that my friend had been bullied, too. The first time I hear he followed me because he liked me but didn't know how to tell me. The first time I realize we were all suffering in our own ways, and we were all a little too oblivious of each other's sufferings. No wonder our parents didn't see what was happening to us. They had to worry about themselves being spied on, or finding a way out of Albania. In the aftermath of the dictatorship, everyone was busy trying to survive. What do you call this tableau? In Picasso's *Guernica*, as an outsider, you're able to see the scale of suffering across all forms of life: animals, children, women, men, buildings. But the ones suffering within can't see any further than their own wounds.

✗

163

The father I have now is so much older than the father who tells me stories in childhood. Back then, he falls asleep mid-sentence, tired after work. He recalls one such instance:

"I hadn't slept for a second or two," he tells me, "when you slapped me across the face demanding 'fol mirë, jo glirë!'"

Fol mirë, jo glirë (Speak clearly, not 'glirë-ly'), where *glirë* is a word I make up to describe the slurred way my father is speaking. The father I have remembers and tells this story with pride. "You see," he says, "you were making poems and translating at the same time since you were three years old, naming things."

The father I have is exactly the father I have always wanted when he knows things about me before they come true and allows himself to see my light and stand within it without impatience or trying to adjust its brightness. The father I have is exactly the father he has always been, from the day we walked together hand in hand to the day his hand slid from mine. "Go home now," he says, "you know the way." For years since childhood, I thought this meant he had abandoned me. It meant he knew I could rely on myself.

When I think of the future, I see my father waiting for me. He is waiting to tell me something. When I reach him, he says: "I am sorry. I wish I had been the father you wanted, the one you most needed. I'm sorry I made you so uncomfortable that you never came to me to tell me what you were struggling with."

The father I have may never say these words to me. It doesn't mean I haven't already forgiven him. It doesn't mean I need his apology to shed my old skin.

SHOOTING STARS

33

"DO YOU MASTURBATE?" Jean asks at one of our earlier sessions.

"Yes, I always have," I answer, a little sheepishly.

"Did you know we masturbate as early as in our mother's womb?"

This I haven't heard before, but I like the specificity of this fact, which indicates that pleasure and desire are what we're born with.

The earliest I remember masturbating is at three years old, playing with toys on the living room floor. I am on my knees reaching both hands to catch something, but I can't reach it so I fall on my right side while my legs get caught pressed together under me. As I keep reaching, I discover that if I rock my body forward and backward, I begin to feel an intense dizzy good feeling. I can't stop until my grandmother sees me and calls to my dad, "O-bo-bo, look what she's doing. Shame! Stop her!"

I understand that the adults don't approve of what I am doing, but I know it feels good, and I learn from this moment that I should keep this knowledge of the body private. Since as a child I will not learn any of Ellen G. White's teachings, I don't find out until my forties that she regarded masturbation as self-abuse. How tragic to be raised afraid to know your own body intimately, to feel guilty when trying to know pleasure, which, along with imagination, is crucial in navigating human experience.

"I've masturbated regularly since," I say to Jean. "Although I grew up religious, I've always felt that this is something I can do whenever I want. I figured early on that God has always wanted me to know what my body is capable of, or that it can do whatever I want it to, and that it is my job to give it space and the chance to surprise me."

"Good for you," Jean says, and then gives me an assignment. The next time I masturbate, she says, I should keep a record of what I fantasize about, things I'm curious about, and then share it with her via email before our next session. Okay, I think. It will be like a creative writing exercise. In college, I would give myself writing prompts in a journal of *secret passions* I'd written in Italian using the Russian alphabet so nobody in my family would understand in case it fell into their hands. It can't be that hard.

But it is hard. I don't want to fantasize. I can't visualize anything because I have no curiosity as to what it would feel like if . . . I never keep the record Jean suggests.

For a long time after Ishan leaves, I feel nothing. When I see Jean and she asks if I have written down any fantasies, or if I can fantasize, I tell her I have no desire to. No image will form in my mind. She practices psychotherapy with me and asks me to take a deep breath and drop down inside myself to let an image arise.

"What comes up for you?" she asks.

Through several of these exercises, I see things in suspension—a stagnant, stuck, ambivalent thing like a white clock placed facedown on the white mantelpiece of an unattended white house, or an anchor simply dangling in amber depths. These objects sit there doing nothing. There is a sense that they will not move, and have no volition.

Days and weeks pass collecting small deaths one after another, the beliefs and hopes I had constructed now deconstructing like a row of dominos. I feel as though I am watching my relationship with Ishan in reverse, so that the last things to let go of are the small rituals with which we first anointed each other—a pair of shorts that fit us both, the sound of his footsteps to the door, prayer bracelets from our first date, and how we tied each other so.

I imagine that trees are learning to remember my face. I am always a visitor, first at the park, then the lake, then from one highway to another, the house a strange warmth I don't know how to wear. The world around me seems to be standing still even as grief has stolen any sense I had of myself. It is all death.

I am grieving the life I thought Ishan and I would have. I am grieving the life I didn't have the courage to get out of when I knew it wasn't good enough for either of us. I can't

It is November, the only time
  rain makes sense—
quiet gray over quiet gray woods
driving the last leaves down the
  unquenchable
eaves and grooves of each street,
down the gullies on the hill,
  down trails
and mountain streams.

start over yet. I don't know then that this is what is happening, why I'm not ready to fantasize. I don't know but my body knows, and I'm grateful to Jean for helping me realize that curiosity will be the first sign to tell me when I am finished with grief.

34

December. January. February—something else is happening to me. I am being noticed by men everywhere I go. A friend of my landlord's asks for my phone number. The checkout man at Trader Joe's, who has never once looked at me, now offers to bag my groceries, chats, smiles. The man who changes my oil flirts with me. A man driving a black Ford truck tells me he loves me. An older man with a Russian accent, who is standing in line with me at the bakery at Whole Foods, tells me I am beautiful. I start going to the gym in tank tops when I didn't dare show my bare arms before. I feel good in my own skin. For once, I feel present in my body and not invisible. I am not afraid to be seen or looked at. The next time I see the new neighbor walking his dog, I make a point to wave, say hi, smile. I have the feeling that I have too much power, that I need to learn to harness it.

And then, in June, I reconnect with my former neighbor, Ben, the guy who taught me how to drive, who tried to kiss me after our one and only date together. My parents have told me his father is ill, and that he has come home to help out. Ben is that same Lenny Kravitz, laidback-sexy, Eagle-Eye-Cherry-save-tonight-and-fight-the-break-of-dawn, long-haired painter he'd been when I first knew him. I like this about him. He doesn't stress about things.

The next time I see Jean, I tell her about him.

"Can you call him?" she asks.

"What? Oh my god!" My hands start to sweat. "I want to. I can't. He'll know why I'm calling."

She laughs and sticks out her tongue at me in a verbless gesture that tells me we both know exactly what I want.

"Do you have his number?"

I remember it even after all these years.

Jean has helped me order a series of dilators, and when I get home, I decide to try them. The first one is a rubbery orange thing about the size of a finger. It looks like a tiny missile, hard enough to not bend, but flexible enough to withstand pressure. I try it, but it's too small. It slips right in and out. I try the second and it's the same. I move to the third, and although it feels pretty comfortable, I decide to take it slower and not rush through this. I tell Jean and she replies:

"I always knew with you it was never a question of *if* but a question of *when*. Take good care of yourself."

Ben's father has passed away around the last week of May and I decide to meet him.

I'm seeing Jean every week this month. We talk about calling Ben. She plays him and I play me. What would I say?

"I'd like to see you. I heard about your father and I'm so sorry. I want to be here for you."

I tell her I feel selfish for why I want to see him. I mention desire, too shy then to even say *sex* at times to her face. She tells me there's nothing wrong with that. The fact that I want to be there for him means I have compassion. "Both desire and compassion are very real, basic, human emotions," she says.

When I leave Jean's office that day, near the door, I'm met with Picasso's "Head of Young Man," an androgynous-looking person with a bald head and black-olive eyes staring straight into mine. It's the way his neck is turned slightly sideways so he can look at me that makes the figure appear alive, as though my presence has caused him to pause and notice me. The head is tilted as though he has just asked a question and is waiting for me to speak. I've always thought the painting is cleverly placed—it's the last thing you see exiting Jean's room—and it acts, for me, like a final check, some inner voice asking, "Did you really mean everything you said today? Did you say everything you wanted to say?"

I find Ben on Facebook and send him a short message. I tell him I don't know what he must be feeling but that I've just come out of a divorce, the process of which has felt like a collection of small deaths. I'd love to see him and be there for him the way I didn't have people there for me.

Two days later, we meet up at a local ice cream place. I watch him turn from the road into the driveway, windows down, long hair in a ponytail. He has seen me and drives over to park next to me. There are his paintings in the backseat—dolphins, mermaids, blue skies, fluffy white clouds, blue water, seahorses.

It doesn't surprise me that he's been doing this for decades and is still at it, and I like that he has such a soft spot for sea creatures. His mermaids are unlike any I have ever seen, their bodies drawn in such a way that they rise from ocean depths in ribbon-like shapes.

We are both beaming ear to ear. He gives me a hug and we get some ice cream and sit by a bush on the grass nearby.

"I'm happy you contacted me," he says. "I met your parents when they came over to see Dad. I asked your mother for your number but she didn't give it to me."

"I know," I say. "She told me."

"So . . . you got married . . . and divorced."

"Yeah." I'm plucking grass and other tiny flowers from the ground as I tell him about my ex. We get up and decide to walk a little path that trails along the woods nearby. He tries to kiss me once, twice, but I push him away or place my cheek on his chest saying, "Not yet, it's too soon." He says, "Look, there's a heron by that swamp right there, see that?" We both crouch, I believe it, and he almost steals a kiss. He's charming, but maybe he's used to getting what he wants. But we are also familiar with one another, so boundaries blur, or seem to dissolve, rather quickly between us.

When he hugs me from behind, he's all arms. His strong arms. I want him. Is that so bad?

We talk about his dad. He doesn't avoid the conversation. Says he's been here for half a year already taking care of his father, trying to help his family. We hang out for about three hours and plan to meet again soon. When we walk to the car, he gives me one of his paintings, a small one of two dolphins swimming upward from blue depths.

The next time I see Ben, he asks me to come by his place where he lives with his mother after she's gone to work. When I get there, he and his black dog Dunkin meet me at the door. I'm inside his house and we're all over each other, plunging into an armchair kissing. His hands are on my thighs, on my breasts, on my butt. I let him. He grabs my hand and draws it to his crotch.

"Oh my god, Ben, your mom will see us. Stop!"

He laughs and pretends there's someone over my shoulder. "Oh, hey, Tom."

"You son of a—" I laugh, and hit him on the shoulder.

We take the dog out for a walk in the woods behind his house. It's sunny but we're shaded. He hugs me from behind. My body likes the heavy feel of a body it wants against it.

We sit on a log that has fallen on the path and talk about something. More kissing. It's like we're both starved. I tell him that. When I have to leave, he walks me to the parking lot, turns me to face my car, pushes me against it, slams his body behind mine and starts to kiss my neck. I feel my legs opening. I drive away knowing all too well what this means.

35

"Ani, have you ever gone into a sex toy shop?" Jean asks during one of our next sessions.

"Yes, once in grad school with a friend," I say, "but all I bought was a book."

"Would it be easier if I went in with you?"

She doesn't have to ask me twice.

We set up a date and I meet her in the parking lot of Brookline's *Good Vibrations*. My hands are sweating. We're going in there to look for a life-sized dildo. They're in all kinds of colors. When I pick the one I'll buy, I am following a memory I have of Ben's size, the one time I saw his body years ago. I buy it. Lube. A book.

Compared to the dilators I had been using until now, the life-size dildo is thicker, longer, harder. Veiny. And it has a life-like head, pee-hole, rim, and everything. At home, I lie on my back and spread my legs. I put lube on me and some on it, too. I pray for a second.

It feels exciting when the head touches me at the opening. It's smooth. But immediately there's resistance, pain. I can't get it in. I manage one inch. That's still a big deal. I have to be patient and take my time with it. Listen to my body better. I remember Jean's words, "good sex needs to be learned and practiced." And I think of the Anaïs Nin quote she probably shared with me the very first day we met: "And the day came when the risk to remain tight in a bud was more painful than the risk it took to blossom."

By now, the grass is so green and the sun's warmth lasts longer on your back if you stand in it. I'm out walking Petey after a night's rain at a state park near our house. I love seeing the trees soaked, their bark charcoal-black, the green—a headrush. The birds draw out the various ways to enter the forest. Their fickle songs couriers of imminent news. I have invited Ben over to my place for dinner. We cook together and he spends the night. We don't sleep at all. We fool around all night long, but I'm not ready yet to go all the way. He knows. He'll wait.

We have coffee in the morning, take a shower together. After he leaves, I notice he has rearranged my flowers and shelves in one of the bookcases in my bedroom. At first, I don't like this—he's not been here longer than a night and he's changing things already. But then I kind of like the idea that someone has the guts to do that—plus, the bookcase looks better.

That morning after Ben leaves, I'm at it again. I insert the largest size dilator breathing deeply, paying attention to how it feels in me, how my own body feels and responds. I have learned in a matter of weeks what I had completely ignored for decades: how to listen to my body and how to tell it to react. All this is coming intuitively now. To the pressure against my skin, I respond with a deep breath. After the deep breath, my body, my flesh relaxes, opens. As I open, I breathe even deeper and recognize I feel good and try to stay in this feeling for an extra moment. To feeling good, I respond with a newfound rhythm. I move the dilator in and out slowly. I visualize moving it sideways and then I experiment moving it sideways. I remember Jean asking me, "What are you curious about?" way back, over a year before all this, when she wanted me to figure out how to fantasize again. I am curious about having an orgasm with someone. To have someone be deep inside me because I want him there. My body responds to the dilator's movements with its own movements and I keep thrusting until I'm all strong convulsions and rippling pleasure.

A few days later, I manage to insert two inches of the dildo. I write to share this news with Jean. She writes right back: "I am smiling as I write . . . would you ever have predicted this?! As always, pay very close attention to what your body is saying. It will never lie to you."

Jean does so much for me with so few words. She is there, supporting my actions and even through the long months when I don't care to change anything. She never tells me, "I know you can do it." She lets that knowledge hover above us in the space we share without mentioning it—I can feel its certainty and believe it in my own time.

Medicine, religion—so many systems in which we place our trust and faith are often too quick to place blame on the woman in a relationship. My father, too: "What do you mean you never had sex?" he says when I tell him years later about my marriage. The notion that sex is natural, that if you can't have it, there's an anomaly that needs to be fixed. People get diagnosed based on symptoms before they're asked to speak openly about their sexuality, their experience, or whether they understand what non-consensual sex is.

Would it be such a radical idea to teach everyone to pay attention to what their bodies are telling them? One of my students once told me something I have never forgotten. The Chinese character for "listen" comprises five elements, the top two of which refer to ears and eyes, listening with our senses; the bottom two to the heart and mind, listening with our soul. And in between these, there's a straight brush stroke that indicates listening with "undivided attention," meaning listening to someone with senses and soul combined and in a focused manner. What if doctors listened when patients said, "I'm not comfortable doing that," and tried, together, to figure out where this language comes from? The cure is in the language. And speaking warrants a listener as much as writing does a reader. What would it take for a patient to feel heard instead of being prescribed the next medication? Instead of having their condition labeled the same way as another patient's in the past? Not every woman who can't have sex has vaginismus. Not every case of vaginismus takes the same length of time or number of dilators and doctor's visits to overcome. Not every woman who can't stand another Pap procedure is being capricious, or needs her hand held, or needs to get it together. We are all different. One size does not fit all.

Maybe it's the very next day, or the same night, or a few days later when I decide to try the dildo again. I want to get this in. So I concentrate on my breathing. I remember how it felt to be weighed down by Ben's whole body pressing against me, on top of me, from behind, from above. *Open, open, open.* I'm chanting in my head, and I don't know where it comes from, but I know this is the moment, this is happening. I don't have to keep repeating *open, open* for too long. It slides in, holy shit, it just did, it's gone in. Okay. Whew, whew. Deep breath. Slowly,

slowly pushing ever so gently now. I'm still on my back, getting turned on. I shift my body slowly, holding on to the base of the dildo from behind me with one hand and balancing my body with the other on the floor. I'm thrusting faster now, about to orgasm, when I lift the dildo slightly toward my back. I feel my flesh stretching there as I orgasm. I relax for a moment, catch my breath, the dildo still inside me, and then I think: Oh god, how do I get this out? I imagine people breaking open my apartment door, days later, because obviously someone would notice I've gone missing. They find me dead on the floor in this position. I can see the headlines:

GIRL DIES WITH FAKE DICK IN VAGINA!

I rotate myself back. The dildo has twisted slightly inside me so it's not exactly in the same angle it was when it went in. Okay. Visualize, focus. Whole babies can come out of here. This can, too. Slowly. Slowly. It's coming out and then, it gets stuck. It's that rim. Dammit. Okay, just breathe. It went in. It will come out again.

I press it to one side of the wall of my vagina. I take another deep breath. Exhale. Breathe deep again. And I feel it come out of me when I exhale, stretching me a little. Oh my god.

36

When I'm ready to tell Ben about all of this, I ask him to go for a walk at Wachusett Reservoir. While we walk, I talk about

Ishan, and I tell him about seeing a sex counselor for a year, about the ambushes in Albania, about being stalked and constantly harassed throughout my adolescence, my fear of men. I confess the rape. It's probably the first time I call it that. To my surprise, Ben responds by making a joke. He says that girls who've gone through much worse would kick my ass if they heard me call it that.

While I'm angry, something prevents me from saying so. We've known each other for years, and I want him to hear this, so I tell him, "There are degrees of violence against women, and they're all wrong. He forced himself on me. The minute you do that, you are raping that person, violating their space, their body, no? Isn't it the same thing?"

It is clear that he doesn't understand. But he's the only person I have been comfortable fooling around with for what feels like a lifetime, and I have been waiting to finally tell someone the truth about my marriage, so I decide to tell him anyway.

We sit on the grass and I take his hands and say, "It's so hard for me to tell you this. You already know, don't you?" I feel like I'm about to cry, although I don't. I'm going to tell another person this huge secret I have lived with for eight years.

"There's no other way for me to say this but to tell you straight out." I'm plucking grass again. "So . . . my husband and I never really . . . consummated our marriage."

"Whaaat?!" His eyes widen.

He is shocked. I think he moves a little. But my hands somehow are back in his hands and he's still holding them. My sweaty hands.

"Yes. I couldn't. I don't think I trusted him. I didn't want to have children with him. It's a lot of things. But we could never do it. We tried but my body completely shut against him. Besides, we were both so inexperienced."

"God, I thought you were going to tell me that you wanted to stop dating," he says. "Wow. I have some big shoes to fill. Poor guy. I feel for him. You should call him. Have you told him all this? How you didn't trust him?"

"No. Not yet anyway," I say, wondering if he would have reacted differently if I had told him how long I had been scared of Ishan.

We sit there quietly for a few moments. Then we lie down, and now he's on top of me and kissing all of my face.

"I want you even more now," he says. "How is this possible?"

I know how, but I don't say anything.

I tell him about the dilators and the dildo. "Funny but the one I picked out is exactly the same size and shape as yours, maybe a millimeter or two smaller," I tell him, and we laugh until that is all you can hear in that field.

In the first week of July, Ben stays over. We kiss and snuggle close for hours until I say, "Okay, I'm ready, but we have to use a condom."

"Okay," he says. "But it's always better without." He winks.

"You're always so charming, aren't you," I say. I hand him the condom and watch him put it on.

I ask him to go very slowly, just let me guide him or just stay there, "at the door"; I will do the moving. I put lube on him and me, lie on my back, and as soon as we touch, I feel my muscles relax, but I'm still anxious and a little skeptical. He's looking me straight in the eyes. There's moonlight, I can see him. He lets me guide him and he's a good listener, so I trust him. He starts to do a sort of "gentle, steady knocking" and I say, "yes, keep doing that but don't go in yet." He doesn't need to do it for long. He lowers his body to kiss me and then he's inside. He thrusts a few times. He comes.

"God," he says, "I came so quickly. I can usually last a long time. You've ruined me."

I don't respond, but I realize, immediately, that this meant two completely different things to us both—to Ben, in that moment, it had been about the performance.

I can hardly believe it. A man was inside me for the first time in my life. I wanted him to be. He wanted to be in me. And it happened. Not like a spell, but in the simplest way I could have imagined. I'm disappointed that it was so quick, so easy. My anxiety and fears peel away. All that I felt during sex with Ben was a strong sense of being fully present. I was never present when Ishan and I tried so many times. I was worried: if it would hurt me; if it would hurt him; if I would get pregnant; if he would like it; if he would want to do it again; if he would want to keep trying again if it didn't happen; if I was driving him mad. Never had I taken the time to stop and think about what *I* was feeling in those moments. What did my body feel? And what did it want or not want to feel? My own flesh. Outside and in.

The next evening, when we try again, we skip the condom, but I ask Ben to pull out before he comes even though I'm on the pill. He knows what I have been through, even though he hasn't fully understood what it has meant or cost me. He'll go as slowly as I need him to. "I know you can do this," he's told me, looking me straight in the eyes, turning on a switch of faith. Tonight, I have the sense that I know what I want my body to do. I want, with all of my selves and all of my pasts, to see what my body *can* do. Ben begins to move slowly in me.

"Do you know how wet you are?" he asks.

I think of the coiled shell that snails retract their bodies into. But there is no shell. There is only my body, moving as though it has always known how, as though it were language, a story, sentence by sentence, a shape, endlessly, knowingly, reshaping.

"Could you have predicted this?" I hear Jean in my head asking, half-teasing, half-thrilled. I'm holding on to Ben's shoulders. Then he tells me to wrap my legs around his waist. He thrusts for a while, then stops. When he does this, I pulse from within and just as I recognize this sensation he thrusts again, faster. We're all rhythm, we're all breathing. He pulls out and comes on my belly and I'm contracting, exploding on the inside. I just want to go again. I look around for a moment. The room is dark. There's only a street lamp, bright enough for me to see Ben's contours above me, my bed, the windows around it. I'm holding one of his hands and wondering what he's thinking, but I don't ask him. I trust him. But mainly, I trust my body. I listen to what it wants. It knows what it wants, and I follow.

A little later, he gets up and turns me face down. My legs spread on their own. He asks me to guide him and I do and tell him to go slowly again. He finds me and moves in ever so slowly, pressing his body tight against mine. He weaves through me. We are a loom. I let him find all of my depth that night. I think of the way dawn weaves through the woods. I hold my breath, and when we come, something cries. I don't know what except I see myself—roots, branches, bark, and all—lifted, dissolved, dispersed; then quietly, ever so slowly, both the night and I reassemble again.

37

All morning long, Ben and I are like children who have discovered mirrors and won't stop shining the sun at each other's faces. Speech is elementary in childhood and it feels that way now. Like a squirrel scuttling around the attic every night, I go back to this memory: There are my feet and he strokes them for the first time. This I will remember. I will also remember that other part—how I bite his shoulder when he comes inside me. It is a new thing to be a pendulum between *the past* and *the future*. With Ben, for a while, time is simply a boat we are on. It matters little where we come from and even less where we are going.

In August, he and I pack a tent in my car and drive up to New Brunswick to see the Bay of Fundy, Nova Scotia, Acadia. We have planned the trip so we will hit the Perseid shower once we're there at a campsite. Ben is calm. When setting up the tent, if we have made a mistake with the instructions, he quietly tries to figure it out, redoing and rotating the edges without getting frustrated. In this he reminds me of my mother, who would advise me to be patient, saying, *Thirri Nevojës!* (Call out to Need!) when I would get frustrated, unable to fix something. Ben has brought some old-school cooking gear. He moves to the side to put it together, lights it up, and begins to make dinner. This is when I think I could live with him. This is when I realize why my grandfather fell for my grandmother the day he first saw her in her backyard.

Sometime before midnight, we get in the car and drive a little farther from the campsite to where it is much darker and you can see the stars clearly. We climb on top of the car and lie there for a while. I have never seen shooting stars until this moment. Not like this. One after another. Not with a man I want to be with, lying next to me. For a moment, I feel sad that I haven't done this until now. And then I remember that I am in it. I am in this moment. This is it. I *am* doing it. I see a star shoot so fast. If I blink I could miss so much. Life is like that. You're here and then you're gone. I don't want to go without burning completely. I grab his hand and squeeze it. He lets me watch and be and doesn't shower me with kisses the way he so often does.

The next day, we walk the shore at Bay of Fundy. The tides here reach up to fifty-six feet, the highest in the world. It's low tide when we arrive so we walk around rock formations and gatherings of seaweed that look like collections of Medusa heads scattered on the shore. I pluck a few of them and sneak them in my pocket. I want to keep this. A moment later, Ben takes out a dollar bill, folds it like a pocket, and stuffs it with sand.

"For your landlady," he says.

Linda loves to collect sand from various beaches around the world—she asks people to bring her some from wherever they go. She must have asked us before we left Framingham. I had forgotten, but he remembered.

He takes photos of me here. Too many, which reminds me of Ishan. I don't want to feel captured, but I brush it off. There is so much to enjoy in these moments.

Thinking of this place now and how those rocks are shaped by the tides, I realize how much this place mirrors my relationship with this man, abundant when the tide comes in, yet still fascinating and perhaps more vibrant when the tide goes out.

I never quite tell him what he means to me, but he's one of those people I know I don't need to explain everything to.

After visiting Bay of Fundy and Nova Scotia, we head south and spend a night in Acadia. We arrive there in the afternoon and decide to catch a sunrise on Cadillac Mountain. We go to bed, wake up at around 3:00 a.m., and drive to the top of the mountain. Ben puts some blankets on the ground in the parking lot and we lie there in the dark. There are very few people out. I see another shooting star. And another. Maybe three that night.

Every time I think of this night, I think of lyrics from my friend Jessica Moore's song, "Shooting Stars": *I drove to the country, saw nine shooting stars / the trees in the night river were blacker than tar / and my life was in the air all around / and stars fell to the ground.*

The air is cold. And my life is and has been in this air the whole summer—I have been thinking of who I was all those years in Albania, who I had become in the years with Ishan, and where I am now with Ben. I am a different person, and yet still me, still attentive to everything around me, aware, always, that where there's beauty, something darker lurks in the periphery. But I will always choose to turn my eyes toward beauty, even as I hold my hand up to feel both. The dark is what makes beauty palpable—I welcome the dark, too.

Ben and I are holding each other. And then you can see the light, ever so faintly. It's as though a lazy painter has taken up the brush and is finally beginning his job, but very slowly, one brushstroke after another. First you see this distant faint light on the horizon that grows pinker, yolkier, orange, bloody orange. You realize soon that the stars have gone out. They are right where they have always been, but you can't see them, almost like this memory now.

Suddenly, I see more people around us and many of us get up and move toward the edge of the mountain, facing the sunrise. It is as if we are in church, voluntarily called by the Holy Spirit to go up to the front and witness. As the firmament lights up, you can see the little islands around Acadia grow more defined. Their contours distinct from one another. They look like stepping stones for some giant being who can pass by here any time now. I wish I were that giant.

A young couple with a little girl moves closer and sits right next to us. We are all from Massachusetts. Ben talks to the father and I can't get enough of this little blonde girl wearing a purple sweatshirt, white heart embroidered on the left side of her chest, black sweatpants with colorful hearts all over them. She holds so much joy, looks me straight in the eyes, and we touch our hands together.

The sun is peeking in at the very edge of the horizon, lifting from the water. First, it looks like a burning caterpillar, longish and thin. Then a moment later it is a bright, bright tooth, halfway out, from an upside-down mouth. Then it is half a pill. And then it is all out. It looks like the sun. The blanket of clouds above us is burning purple pink. I take a photo of the little girl. I count at least ten stepping stones behind her. She waves at me. This is the first time I catch myself thinking I might like to have a child.

38

Ben and I date for a year. But I don't really call it dating, and I don't call him my boyfriend. I realize I am not serious with him, which is a first for me. He doesn't seem serious either. He is an artist; he can pick up and go whenever he wants. I love this about him. This is what he has chosen for himself. He often talks of how much he wants to take off and live off the grid. In fact, he has mostly done that all these years.

I'm realizing that I'm looking for someone I want to be with long-term, and that I don't see this happening with Ben. I sense a lack of intentionality with him but that's what I want from someone. I sense a pulling apart, coming mostly from me, which hurts because he's meant so much.

I have never broken up with someone before. Yes, I have divorced, but that was different, and Ishan was the one who initiated it. I begin to understand a little of what Ishan must have gone through in preparing to tell me that he was leaving.

I take Ben to the reservoir, our favorite place, to tell him. It is June again. A year later, and the grass is green. I have brought some strawberries for us to eat and we decide to sit down on the grass near a transmission tower. I'm a year older than the woman who told him what she couldn't imagine telling anyone. I pluck at the grass.

"You know how you've been my first everything? First kiss. First fuck . . . " We laugh. "Well, I've never done what I'm about to do now either. . . . I even think your father had something to do with us finding each other again," I say. "Maybe that was his wish. But . . . I don't see us going much further." I manage to blurt it out, fingering leaves of grass, making knots and knots into each as if trying to bind something I would soon come to know had no business being captured.

He smiles and seems very understanding. He does that so well. Looks at me through the whole thing. Doesn't show sadness and yet I feel sad.

"I know," is all he says and keeps looking at me. He takes my face in his hands and kisses me once for a long couple of seconds. Then he stands up, takes the strawberry stems we'd discarded, and buries them in the soft square of earth inside

187

the open legs of the transmission tower we had been sitting next to.

We walk back to my car. We are still smiling and joking like normal. It doesn't feel like we have just broken up. It feels like when you cut yourself and it takes a while before you notice the pain. I give him a framed photo of the little girl we met on top of Cadillac Mountain during the sunrise almost a year ago.

At home, later that evening, as I rub my earlobe, I notice I no longer have one of my amber earrings. How lovely, I think—that breaking up with Ben, I lost an earring somewhere on a raised field, at the foot of a transmission tower, sandwiched right in the middle of energy lines above and water's course below. This whole year I had with him—something of a firefly, something of a blinking star—I'll always know where it is.

DESIRE

39

IN FEBRUARY 2013, I publish my first book of poems, *Bread on Running Waters*, through Fenway Press, a small independent publisher. Its founder, David Gullette, has always encouraged and supported my writing at Simmons University. The press is small and has no marketing team; after publication, there are no reviews of my book. Almost two years later, I reach out to poet Andrea Cohen, who is the director of the Blacksmith House Poetry Series in Cambridge, to introduce myself and pitch a reading with another poet. She agrees. And finally, this poetry—this bread thrown onto the water, like the Bible said, like my grandmother often reminded me—begins to come back to me in small, meaningful ways. I let all my friends and contacts know about the event via Facebook.

A day or so later, a man I know from the gym sends me a message:

"Ani, I noticed you're giving a poetry reading in Cambridge on the 8th. I've often been curious about such readings and since I know the poet I thought I'd come hear you if you don't think that's weird."

This is interesting, I think.

I have known Jai for almost three years now, though I hardly talk to him. He seems so serious all the time. I don't think he ever even smiles at me. And now he writes to me through instant messenger? Okay, I write, sure, that would be awesome.

I meet Jai at a café around the corner from Blacksmith House before the reading. It strikes me how calm he is. I am already curious about what made him want to come hear me read. But I don't ask him. I'm just glad he'll be there. He might be the only person I know in the audience and this comforts me. I realize as he enters the café that I am noticing him for the first time. I haven't looked at him in the gym other than as another athlete, and he is an athlete, perfectly proportioned. He can't be any taller than I am, and he weighs less than I do: muscled, toned, his head completely shaved. When I look at him, I think of the Oscar statue: small, tight, acrobatic. One of those men you imagine could lift, balance, and spin the whole world on their index finger.

The reading goes well. Knowing that Jai is there hearing this most personal side of me makes me feel something powerful. Afterward, I talk to friends who have come and a few people who want to talk to me or buy my book. Jai is standing at the end of the room, checking his phone, waiting for me.

When we leave together, it has just started to snow.

"How did you like it?" I ask.

"It was good. You did well. I have a lot of respect for people who put themselves out there like that," he says, and I notice that I hadn't really thought of this before. We do put ourselves out there. As writers, we never know how the audience will react, but we read to complete strangers things we've written in private.

We have parked at the same garage—in fact, our cars are not that far from each other.

"You have a good night," he says, and we shake hands.

A week later, we meet at a Thai restaurant near the gym.

I don't remember what we talk about, only how Jai looks at me. I feel like he can see beyond my physicality, right into that ungraspable self, beneath the flesh and bones. I feel a strong attraction. It is December. I haven't been with anyone since June, when I broke up with Ben. So maybe I am just horny, I tell myself, but all I can see that night are Jai's eyes like two black shining wells, pulling me in. I try to hold his gaze a few times. But I feel shy and don't hold it for long. I'm afraid he reads me too well and knows that I'm attracted to him.

There is a pre-Christmas potluck party at the gym and we decide to go, not exactly together, but to hang out, and then afterward go for a drink just the two of us. The party is mostly uneventful, but someone is taking photos, and when Jai and I are in the kitchen fixing a drink and talking to some of our other friends, the woman with the camera comes and clicks a photo of us: the first and maybe only one of just the two of us. It's striking to me how happy we look, even more striking that the happiness on my face resembles his. We have the exact same smile, same half-moon lines framing our lips, both our lips parted, lit brown eyes, same leftward tilt of the head, same height too, except that he's perfectly bald and I have Medusa hair.

A day or so before this party, I learn that Jai is divorced and has two grown children.

I don't know it at the time, but my anxiety is getting the best of me. Call it anxiety. Call it listening to other voices in your head instead of your own. The thought of dating Jai reminds me of the time I first entered Ishan's home in Orissa and couldn't stop crying. I realize now that in both instances, I was worried about what my mother would think before I could give myself time to navigate the relationship on my own terms. I tell Jai I'm not ready for a relationship.

Sometime that winter, Jai invites me over to his place for dinner. He says he will leave the door open, "just come right in." I am drawn to someone who opens himself to me. I was drawn to India in the same way, to Thailand, and many years later, to Ireland and another man I met there. So I enter, go up a set of stairs to the top floor. There are antlers on the wall facing the stairs. Some music. Someone is cooking; I hear sizzling. For a moment I think, wow, he hunts?! But soon find out he rents here. The antlers came with the house. I am always so quick to build stories from details and I'm so often off. But just as often, I am right, too, when I pay closer attention. I trust this hyper-imagination I have even if, at times, it leads me astray.

Jai is making bhindi, my favorite vegetable, and some beef stew. Dinner is delicious. We drink wine. Listen to more music. Talk about everything. We move to the living room to watch a movie. Pretty soon, we're lying on the couch together and we start to kiss. I am shy and super conscious that I may not be good at this. I tell him this and he says, "I'm crazy about you." Is it the wine or is it the words I didn't know I wanted to hear? I'm already kissing him, becoming all feeling. I like this thing he does where he kind of buries his whole head into mine. His lips pressing against mine, pushing my head one way, mine pressing and pushing right back.

"Stay here tonight," he says.

I want to, but I think of Petey. I have never left him alone at night. I have fed him dinner and taken him out for the night. But he must be waiting for me.

"Stay here," he says a second time. I feel disarmed. He knows exactly what he wants. I know what I want and I'm nervous. I don't know him all that well, but I completely trust this man— my hands aren't even sweating. I trust his language, which is short, to the point. He does not waste words. He also says what he wants, comes right out with it, no games or second-guessing, nothing to read between the lines.

I want to stay.

"Petey will be fine," he says. "You can go back early in the morning."

He turns the light off and we slip into bed toward each other like darkness, velvety and warm. There is nothing in the room but our bodies nearing each other, arching, softening, becoming erect. We stay up nearly all night holding and kissing each other, feeling what the other feels. All my senses alert. All of his. In the dark, it feels like together we become one eye except even the eye doesn't see, it just feels. We don't have sex, neither of us even says we will or we won't, and yet I have never experienced this shared oneness before. In the morning, he tells me he hadn't either. I have never felt so aware of my body.

The next time I see him, when we go to the bedroom, I say, "We don't have to do it tonight," by which I mean I don't really want to have sex, I'm not ready, but he doesn't know that's what I mean and then we're in bed, already naked somehow, and the light from the hallway is bouncing off his head and I can see his contours but I can't see his face, which bothers me, it's like I'm having sex with a shadow, although I don't tell him, because I don't want to ruin it.

If I could go back, this is the only thing I would change, in any relationship: to wait. Even when you know you want to be that intimate with someone. If there's a small voice that says "wait" inside you, listen. Instead, in this moment, I feel a split between my mind and my body. My body is into it, but my mind is thinking, "This isn't right. It's too soon." He is inside me very quickly and I'm thrilled about that—so it wasn't just Ben, I can actually still do this—but also I have to get out of here.

"I need to leave," I say as soon as we're done. "I can't stay."

I didn't like it. It felt selfish of us both. Like we both needed to see what sex would be like. Like he needed to confirm my story, or maybe I had needed it. I didn't like it and wanted to get out of there and I did.

He surprises me later by reminding me that this is our first time, that most first times can be awkward, like a first kiss, because you don't know what the other person likes yet, maybe not even how you like to do things around this person.

"It's a time to explore, not to evaluate," he says. He is telling me that I should at least relax and give it another try. And we do give it another try, and another, and another, and every time it is either better, or new, or strange, or exciting.

Jai is confident and full of energy. He can strike up a conversation with anyone: a bartender, someone on the sidewalk, at a concert, anywhere. He introduces me to his son one day over speaker phone when they are out together hiking in Utah. Same thing with his daughter, ex-wife, and parents, face-to-face, matter-of-fact, *boom*, no fuss, just throws me to them and vice versa, a sink-or-swim kind of attitude.

I like him when he is vulnerable, something he rarely lets me see. When he shares with me what it is like to be a parent, I realize things about my own parents I hadn't thought of before. Jai's daughter will graduate from high school in two years, and he has started to take her to visit college campuses so she can see for herself and make up her own mind, something my parents could have never afforded for my brother and me. "She'll be going so far away," he says. "Do you know what it was like when my son moved to California for college? It broke my heart. Your heart is literally plucked out when your child moves that far away. I don't know how your parents did it when you left to go to Thailand, all the way across the world."

It hasn't occurred to me until this moment that my parents might have been hurting. I knew they had worried if I would be okay or not. I knew they would miss me; that was expected. But pain? I never thought about it. As Jai and I talk about our families, where our people originated, what they'd gone through, I realize for the first time what it meant that as soon as my parents settled in this country, as soon as I graduated with a masters' degree, I left. Many people do this. Setting off, spreading their wings, exposing themselves to another culture. It's just that I always saw it as a brave act on my part. It never occurred to me that my parents were probably a little braver, never confessing once how such a decision must have affected them.

It is these seemingly small things that make me want to get to know Jai more deeply. Like how he cooks, always tasting the food for salt; how he makes room for music in the evenings and lets it pool into and around the space between us where we sit sipping wine, running through song lists the way one runs through a photo album. I love the windows in his house, not because of the light, but because he keeps them open. That and the fact that he grows plants are probably the first things I notice that I like about him. In his house, sunlight, the breeze, the dust move in through his walls and floors, gently, taking their time to settle in for a while and then with more time, gone, as if they'd never been. It is the first time I notice a man who has aligned his sense of self with his house. His house is a universe where nothing is final, where everything belongs.

I like him on top of me when he moves inside me going in, coming out. Slow. Then slower at first, pinning one of my arms above my head with his resolute hand, his dreaming hand dipping two fingers in my mouth, then his mouth doing a hummingbird trajectory between my lips, one nipple, then the next, and my neck, back and forth, in no order, but exactly in the order that leaves me breathless as he thrusts faster, so wet that I can hear us, his in, his out, in, out, my giving in over and over to completely rippling open. That he knows when to slap me. When not to. Yes. Harder. "God," he says when he comes. Or maybe I say it.

40

Massachusetts is hit by at least six blizzards the first three months of the year. Jai and I time them so that Petey and I either get snowed in at Jai's or he will be at my place.

Petey likes Jai, but I have a sense that something is slipping away, that Petey will leave me. I notice soon enough that he is peeing a lot whenever we go out for walks. He pees and pees into the snow banks on the street. He drinks a lot of water, all the time. One day I notice he is licking himself too intensely on his butt, something he usually does when his glands won't express well. Then I notice some blood on the floor—and when I check him, I see he has a little wound.

Sometimes after we make love
our warm bodies lying naked in a cool dark
your palm a light hope on my bare back

It is the last week of February.

The vet feels around the wound and can already tell that it is cancer. She does a biopsy and the results will come out in a few days, but she is up-front with me from the start that Petey has an aggressive tumor. She prescribes painkillers

and my face away from you
you don't know that I'm crying.
I am thinking then of Petey

and something to help with the liver, which she says is being affected, why he is drinking and peeing so much.

I am shattered. Petey is only eight years old.

"How much longer will he have?"

She can't give me an answer.

how much I miss him.

"You never know for sure with these cases," she says. It could be weeks. It could be months. But it is clear that I don't have many options. My Petey, who has been through so much with me, who was so difficult to train at the beginning, whom I grew to love hard, is not going to be around for long. It hurts to hear this. I drive home with him, get him out of the car while I am talking to my brother on the phone, and leave my keys in the car running, locking ourselves out of both car and house. Jai drives over and brings me coffee. We wait for AAA to come and unlock my car. Then, in the house, I can finally cry.

After the diagnosis, I have six weeks left with Petey. The first batch of medications make him feel better for a while. The wound dries up and seems to be doing better. When my brother, his wife, and my parents visit, he is like old times, playing with them and being his happy self. When they leave, he is lethargic again. Then he starts skipping a few meals and not eating his kibble anymore. He will only eat rice and other cooked food or treats.

One night I have a dream where he is talking to me in a language that is not any language I speak, but one I intuitively understand. He is saying, "What's the point of these pills? I don't want them," and his face looks uncomfortable and unhappy. I wake up crying. It is the end of March.

Petey has started to moan now sometimes in the evenings. The tumor has grown so that each time he relieves himself I can see the shape of it is flatter—the pressure from the tumor is making everything more difficult. He can still go on walks, still gets excited when Jai comes over, but he isn't himself.

I remember when I had to put him down
he came to sit on my lap

I take him out for a nice long walk, over an hour, because it is so warm and sunny out. He enjoys it, but he is a little slower than usual and doesn't pull on the leash, though he is pretty strong throughout the whole walk. After we're home, he starts drooling. Later that afternoon, he lies in the bathroom for a few hours. Not his usual place at all. Shaking and still drooling. I talk to his vet via email and decide that he is feeling weak from a combination of walking for too long, not having eaten all day, and not having taken his Rimadyl that morning. I force Rimadyl down his throat there in the bathroom. Soon afterward he is able to eat again and the shivering and salivating stop.

Two days later, I take Petey out after I come home from work. We don't walk much at all but when we get back in the house, he starts shaking again. I take him straight to the clinic. A new vet sees him and tells me that the tumor has grown into a U shape around his anus. She prescribes tramadol, which will make him more lethargic, she says, but will keep him comfortable. I hate the idea of stuffing him with more medicine. What's the point? If he's not fully himself, am I not being selfish keeping him around through medication? I can feel what I have to do. It is standing behind me, I have to just turn. The inevitable is right there.

and the vet and I decided
   not to move him
so she injected him then
and I held him as he fell

so slowly sideways
all ninety-five pounds of him
almost too softly

I know the next day that I have to put Petey down. He still has his good hours, but is mostly sleeping throughout the day, eating mainly treats and yogurt. He won't pull me anymore on the leash. I decide I don't want to wait much longer, don't want to see him get any weaker. I want to say goodbye to him when he can still know me and feel me the way he has always felt me. The way I have always seen him: goofy, strong, beautiful, a handful of a dog, Petey.

that it seemed he was forever leaving
relaxed muscles, relaxed bones
until he reached the floor

and I couldn't hold him close enough
anymore
and felt an untying

I go to bed that night feeling that Saturday is the day. I wake up to heavy rain and lightning and then doubt myself about the timing, but once Petey wakes up, everything falls into place. He sits by his favorite window in my bedroom paying attention to the cars driving by, patiently and quietly sitting with his beautiful black head and full black back that always remind me of my grandma, reading her Bible on her bed with her black coat on in the winter because we had no heat. His face is perfectly divided in half, straight down the middle, so that he is pure white on the right side and pure black on the left. That soft white belly with black dots, his strong chest where the hair from all sides gathers into a whorl, my favorite spot. He lets me know in so many ways that this is the day, the right time, and I feel him fuse me with strength and a strange joy.

My sister-in-law comes over. I have asked her to be with me, and together we go for a walk to Petey's favorite park. Later, he inhales a whole McDonald's cheeseburger along with soft-serve ice cream. The day is all kinds of weather, but he is so into everything that we are doing. At the vet, he is kissing and

so quick
but so slow I knew then
endless strings had bound us

and when I breathed in
he was gone
as if I'd breathed him in.

playing with everybody but me. Then, after what seems like hours, he comes and sits on my lap, where he stays.

At Jai's that night, I cry and cry into his chest. He holds me and tells me to cry as much as I want. I will miss Petey every day for weeks, months, a full year. Whenever I think of him now I miss him the same.

Sometimes after we make love
after we lay down
and rest

even when I'm turned away
I'm holding on to you
with all of my hands.

I am holding on to Jai and I don't see at the time what this resembles. Once

201

again, as with Ishan, I am pinning my happiness on the presence of a man in my life, someone I half hold on to while half waiting for him to choose me. At the time, I don't yet know that true happiness, whether with or without someone else, comes from the freedom to make choices on your own terms.

41

My body. Have I loved you yet? Your tiny wrists. Your not-so-elegant ankles. Your thighs with those few stretch marks on the sides like wave ripple marks on the sand. Your crooked bottom teeth. Your sweaty palms. Have I held on to you yet? You are my life. My life is a whole universe. I am the only God I can get up close and personal with.

Later, when the entire world is devastated by a pandemic, we will spend those years alone together, just you and I in the apartment I lived in with Ishan. When I stop by a mirror, there you are. This new form of you, larger, stocky, plumper all around like most bodies now. I stand in the shower and hold on to my love handles and flex. How did this butt get so firm? What is it like for the body when I have to teach full-time, revise a book in its final stages, take care of my aging parents and friendships, all the while recognizing that no one is around to do my dishes, no one but me to buy groceries or wash the laundry or give me a back rub or a full-body massage, no one to vacuum or take out the trash or wash the mirrors and windows, no one to sweep the stairs or mail things off for me, all the bureaucratic red tape and taxes I've always done on my own, no one but you carrying me through it all. Some nights an elephant sits on my chest.

The doctor recommends Lexapro. I give it a try and feel it working that first week. It is a presence, as though an invisible fishnet made of the silkiest gossamer is cast over my emotions to rein them in. I feel captured, or rather that my feelings have been caught and are being held ever so gently in this net made of the thinnest of threads. I move through the hours without stress or fear. Is this what Petey felt when the vet put him on tramadol, the pain seemingly being vacuumed out of his body? I recognize I'm still my usual content self, but six months fly by, and twenty-five pounds later, I realize that I haven't cried once.

The invisible gossamer has woven itself slowly, inwardly, building intricately, undetectably like icicles on the windshield overnight: they're not there at night, and in the morning you can't see anything but. When I get off Lexapro, I know I am coming back to myself through tears that return, through my ability to mentally jump years into the future before I take a first step now.

But during the time on Lexapro, I feed and spoil you and remove you from the privilege of going to the gym because something has to give. I eat lazy breakfasts I can take my time with at 5:30 a.m. so I can report to work by 7:00. Sometimes I eat breakfast for dinner, too, and my cholesterol sneaks up the chart. I see it manifesting on my belly that has grown two rolls. I hear it in my lungs when they struggle for a deep breath—I sound like my father when I tie my shoes.

I wake and sit up on the bed, a long mirror facing me. I lift my shirt to see the shape of my belly. I feel a slight shame that I keep checking myself out like this, wishing the pounds would magically disappear. I'm already a size large, and I keep buying medium-sized clothes. Then my friend Sara reminds me, "Your body has taken you through this pandemic! Love it! Talk to it in the mirror!"

How do I approach something I have had no time to tend to in a long while? How do I return to it? Like the country I have long stayed removed from, will it welcome me back? Will we speak the same language?

Yes, home welcomes you right back. In returning to it, I imagine the path like approaching the snail shell of my own inner ear. Meandering and spiraling first in my mind toward you. Spinning out thoughts around your outer edges as I make my way to the mirror in the bedroom to see you. This is how I know one day I will be okay with reaching home. "Hi." I begin to speak to you in the mirror now. "Thank you for never locking your doors on me." I take my eyes off the reflection in the mirror and see my body through the body. I hear my heartbeat in my ear, I feel my veins and my blood pressure slightly raised. I listen for the nerve endings of my body and the nerve endings of my return home to merge into one. The body says: *Here. I am here. We are here together. I will be here even when I no longer have shape or form.*

Here, I say back to it. *Thank you for holding me so close.*

42

Several months after Petey passes away, I am climbing Sulphur Mountain in Canada, aiming for the gondola. I have come here for a translators' residency. And here, among the mountains, I am reminded of my smallness. Of how I became a translator years before, of works written in my mother tongue into English, even though I am still not 100% at home in this target language. When I turned thirty, I sought revenge against the country I thought had failed to recognize my work. I snuck into translation's belly like men once did into the Trojan Horse. But I was no Odysseus, just an ordinary female soldier no one could make something out of. From within the horse's belly, I saw how, suddenly, there was interest in the work I was creating. Suddenly, I won an award and doors began to open.

I had tasted something like this before, when pushing myself to pass for a native speaker all those years in college and graduate school. When I had to prove myself time and again to male co-workers that I was qualified to teach English as a Second Language as much as they were. That I was a published author even though English was not my first language. That I would have to tell the retired teacher who volunteered as a substitute at our school to stop referring to me as "kid" or making announcements like "here comes the poet" when I joined everyone at the lunch table.

"What a bitter woman!" he responded, and I've never been prouder to tell someone off. But not until now that I have chosen to translate does it become real for me, the extent to which an immigrant writer must be a shapeshifter.

I am a shapeshifter by choice and translation is part of my identity. Translators build bridges between cultures, languages, and the art of writing. They're also known as midwives, literary tradition influencers, mediators, seers. My favorite time to write is just before it gets fully dark. I love to sit on the floor in my home just as the lights in the sky dim and I do not turn on the lights. I am writing with the same speed of the falling dusk and in those moments, just as I can still make out the shapes of everything in my room and just before it gets too dark to sit without the lights on, I have written some of the best poems that come to me fully formed. My pen and mind are in tune with the shifts and journey of light. I know I have arrived at a completed poem or translation when I have traveled through diction, as through that dusk, toward an inner brightness. My heart feels lighter, lifted, when I know I am done.

If we're lucky, there's something to learn from following one's smallness, because we cannot predict where we might land in the process of the chase. The more I translate, the more I find pleasure in it—the process resembles that of revision I am familiar with. I struggle with many word choices and listen deeply to unpuzzle the lines, to bring out the author's voice much like when I try to find my own. But more than anything, I have learned to not judge myself so harshly. It wasn't my smallness that guided me, although it did knock on that door. But once I began translating from my mother tongue, it became clear how much I had longed for it, having lived the majority of my life till then around an Albanian language that arrived broken to my ears and tongue. Here I was, reading an Albanian that sung and no longer restricted me. Here was a language that spoke to my soul. I couldn't not share it.

I am at the residency, in the midst of the Canadian Rockies, precisely because my translations have been valued. I have not been near such tall, numerous mountains since my childhood in Albania. Once here, I feel a complete stranger and, therefore, immediately at home. I make lifelong friends here, people I treasure to this day.

At first, I'm taken by the sheer number of mountains that spread out before us. Mountains, I think to myself, are never lonely. They have each other the way my newly made friends and I sharpen one another's experience here, strengthen it. One thing feels different. Although I am facing ageless, immense wilderness, I do not feel truly small. I belong. I have my own presence. If the residency gives me anything, besides time to sit, translate, and revise, it is exactly this—presence. Here, I feel most defined. Like the contours of who I am and who I can become are finally etched in permanent marker. I begin and end with me and, in that circuitous route, I carry with me everyone and everything with which I have crossed paths.

One afternoon, we go on a hike with a guide who tells us that Tunnel Mountain, at the feet of which our residency is located, is actually known as Sleeping Buffalo to First Nations people like the Stoney Nakoda and Blackfoot. They used to come here on vision quests and other ceremonies. They had named the mountain Sleeping Buffalo because it resembles one when seen from Sulphur Mountain. The First Nations people believed this mountain was sacred.

"When you sleep here," the guide says, "pay close attention to your dreams. You could receive a vision the buffalo grants you."

I don't remember if I ask for a vision that night before going to bed, although I think about the guide's words.

I fall asleep and see myself in a place that seems to have been my home, and suddenly a large blue fish comes flowing in, half his body in the living room and the other half in the bedroom, it is enormous. It travels slowly from one space to another and because he is so big, I can only look at half his body at a time. Light bluish-green. Scales. He moves in from one room to my right and out the other to my left. Then returns facing me, but when he approaches, he has transformed into a tall, towering bird that comes to sit on my lap. Exactly what Petey did before I had to put him down. I have a similar feeling of comfort, of things being right and how they should be, which he had also given me in those moments.

What fascinates me about this bird as it stands tall above me, its head to the ceiling, is that its whole body is covered in intricate designs. Its body is not made of flesh, but an iron structure of sorts, like a ship, and covered in mosaics. The creature says nothing to me, but it clearly feels most present and marks me in some way. The whole dream feels like a visit. Throughout, I keep thinking I don't recognize this bird from anywhere in the animal world I know. What species is it?

It is not until the next day, when I come across some paintings of ravens by Native Americans in the shops downtown, that I recognize the bird I had dreamed. The bird I had seen was all black, with a tribal-like design and a body full of carved details like the one in front of me at the shop. I am thrilled to find out the symbolic meaning of a raven, the trickster, a shapeshifter, the one that stole the sun so everyone could share it. Its gifts are known to be knowledge and creativity, clarity and transformation.

I think of a James Allen quote: "Dream lofty dreams, and as you dream so you shall become." I have felt the raven's gifts. The ability to speak and keep an open mind. Break free.

Evolve. The desire to share my story. I have known these gifts.

On the last day, I board the airport shuttle alone. Most of the other translators left earlier in the morning or the day before. On the ride to the airport, the farmland and fields are speckled with cows and horses for miles and miles—everything seems to have come out to graze as I am leaving this place. A journey punctuated by this bounty of living things feasting on sweet earth. I can't write a book about all I felt through this journey the way my camera can't capture the mountains that my eyes saw. But I know it was real. As real as the cold, jade-colored river water at my feet. I felt incredibly blessed, present, grateful to God.

43

Coming back from the Canadian residency, under the spell of those mountains, I begin to write a book. I also write a poem about being a mountain, asking someone to change me the way the sun, fire, rain, ice, and wind change a mountain, carrying it to the sea a million years and a particle at a time. I am in love, idealizing the world. I have continued to be good at pinning my own happiness on another man changing me, making me feel beautiful. For the longest time, I have believed that my full transformation depends on how someone loves and sees me.

It is a gift to be seen. But I don't yet recognize that being seen comes from changing within. I have lived for so long never forgetting how Albania changed me. I see in Jai the person I could have been if my past had been different. And I'm still running with the fantasy that he can transform me, not unlike how I believed I could help Ishan. Have I learned nothing? Or is learning much more complex and circuitous than comparing present mistakes to past ones?

"Why do you let Jai, or anyone, tell you a fairytale that has nothing to do with who you are?" Jean asks me when I tell her that Jai thinks I don't push myself hard enough.

"I don't know; maybe he sees who I might become?"

She doesn't respond to that, something I have come to understand as her way of making space for me to hear what I have just said so I can reflect on it further, maybe so I can hear the untrue story I was telling myself again. But I am uncomfortable hearing what is true at this moment and switch the conversation to how I make myself small in public.

"Why do you think you do that?"

"Maybe I'm uncomfortable with attention?"

"You don't want to rock the boat, but that's an adaptive behavior turned into a habit," Jean replies. "It's your self-effacing persona that helped you get through the circumstances you were living in then."

She pauses.

"But you have a right to be who you are," she adds, and then assigns me to pay attention to every time I giggle and see if I find a pattern.

There has been a pattern. I would always do it, had done it, sometimes still do it, when I recognize my power in a social situation and want to tone it down, to shift attention away from myself. Giggling is how I have learned to give my power away, be it in connection to Jai, a colleague, my friends, my parents, my brother.

In the poem I wrote, the speaker feels enough power to be a mountain and yet, in the same breath, she believes it's another's ability to change her that can fully transform her into the mountain she knows she is.

It has taken me time to know myself. To know, too, that transformation has to come from within for there to be a story to tell.

When Ishan and I were together, we had this understanding— we were always able to share everything. We believed that where one of us ended the other began and that made us one. There were no boundaries between us.

In the relationship with Jai, things are different. He cares for other people who are not me. He has his children. His parents.

211

An ex-wife. Ex-girlfriends. All of whom he maintains meaningful relationships with, people he still respects and values, and meets with often. He has his friends and business partners he goes out with from time to time, and for whom he will be there if they need him. We are talking about this when he points out that I do not have any of this.

"You do not have friends," he says. "Not more than a handful, anyway. If you were to go through something terrible right now, whose number would you pick up and call?"

I can think of my brother, his wife. But that's about it. Even opening up to my parents seems like something I won't, can't do. They have had enough troubles. I am getting close to my friend Sara around this time. Maybe her. Maybe other friends I haven't spoken to in a while because of recent transitions.

"How did you get through your divorce? I can't imagine how you did that all by yourself."

"I had Jean," I say, "and my brother and his wife to some extent. I had my book of poems that was about to be published . . . The woman from Cambridge I met on the plane."

"Do you know which relationship has been the most meaningful to you? The deepest one you've ever had? You probably don't even know it yourself," he says with that all-knowing air about him which I half like because it usually reveals something I hadn't thought about in that way, and half hate because I often feel measured, the way he carefully measures salt when he cooks.

"What do you mean? With my parents?"

"Petey," he drops the name out of nowhere and it is like a spell. He's saying the most meaningful relationship in my life, so far, has been with a dog. Not another human. But with someone I adopted, cared for, taught to walk gently with me, cried with when he was hit or yelled at by my ex, watched get all excited over a few guys I introduced him to after Ishan, took swimming even though I'm scared shitless of being in the water.

"Yes, Petey," he says. "Did you ever forget to feed him? Did you ever forget to take him out?"

No, I was always there for him. I was with him to the very end. He is right. But my grandmother had been another. And she, like Petey, has always been with me. He is right, but only for a moment. He cannot know, in the year or less that he has known me, of all the friendships in my past or those to come. This thing we do: speaking with the certainty that we know better than the other person what's best for them, and calling it care. He thinks he knows me. But relationships evolve. I have been there for others in ways I don't need to measure to convince anyone else of their meaningfulness.

I'm in the living room at Jai's place, sitting on the couch. We're watching a movie. I move over to where he is and put my head on his lap, my breathing already changing. Soon, I turn my head and kiss his groin and suddenly the room falls quieter. He lets out a slow breath and I feel him grow harder under the cloth under my mouth. I kneel on the floor facing him and hold his entire pelvis with my hands as if it were a large bowl I'm about to drink from. I pull down his pants. "I love your dick." My mouth names it. It is so clean and perfectly shaped. I bless it with my eyes, looking at it for a slow moment. I bless it with my breath as I bow over it, with my tongue and my whole mouth, I bless it all the way down, up and down again, to its base. I suck him until he comes into my mouth. I let him.

When I ask him later, "Why didn't you stop me? Why didn't you ask if you could come in my mouth?" he says, "I had a feeling you were going to go all the way this time." It surprises me because I, too, knew I was going to and didn't want to stop. I was so turned on by the fact that I was the one who initiated it and that he didn't stop me. The turn-on had come from wanting something he didn't ask for, didn't guide me toward. It is the same feeling I'd had four years before, in the car, when I gave myself an orgasm while driving. This was desire. Pure, unadulterated. Unstoppable.

This is my body aware of itself, when I go to someone I desire, when I feel empowered and trust someone I want and allow them to see me. Someone there's no end to the ways in which I would allow them to see me. This is how I follow desire, another language I've become fluent in.

In some ways, writing this book is a way of naming different forms of love. How I came to know desire. Later in life. Much later. I did not survive girlhood. I avoided it. And when womanhood arrived, I was unprepared to recognize it. I wrote this book so that the words from the pages of that time in my life would finally assemble, and I would speak. And I would see myself. Because language is a presence, and to speak means to be seen.

44

Friends. They are the people you can be yourself around. You know them by their attention. They ask questions. They don't hold back their stories. When they listen to you, the conversation seeps into the fabric of your past and future lives—they will always be a part of you.

It's Sara's birthday and a group of us decide to rent a little cottage on the Cape together—my friend Mer, her husband, our friend Kristiana, Tim and Sara, and I.

Sara's from Iran and has lived in the States for more than ten years. She's seen her family maybe twice since she left. She's the one everyone notices, not just because she's all retro-model, I-don't-buy-new-stuff-I-reinvent-what-I-find type of genius, has a magical laughter that knocks down doors, the calmest wise words at the right time, and a unique style you want to copy and keep up with—although she is all of those things. She's the one everyone notices simply because of how she breathes and moves in the world: she is music. You hear people like her long before you see and get to know them. And on this night, when it is time to exchange gifts, Tim brings out a big box that everyone thinks is a huge jigsaw puzzle because it kind of rattles in that way. Sara gets all excited and starts tearing up the edges.

"Be careful," Tim warns her, pleased with her excitement.

So she slows down and we begin to realize this isn't a jigsaw puzzle at all. What is this box, square like a pizza box but slightly thicker?

When she opens it, to everyone's surprise, especially Sara's, we see that it is a Daf, a Persian hand drum made of goatskin with beautiful Persian calligraphy drawn on it like a tattoo and three or four rows of metal ringlets attached all around the inside—when you shake and beat it, the rings add their own sounds to the *dap dap dap* of the drum.

"Aaaaaaaaaaahhhhh! Ahhhhhhh!" she screams in her Sara way, full of all kinds of emotions—is she crying, is she laughing, is she happy, is she grieving?

"Where did you get this? Oh my god! How did you know?"

Tim just smiles standing there watching her, speechless. All of us, huge grins on our faces.

She used to play Daf when she was young back in Tehran, she tells us. So she plays it now. She pauses for a moment before starting, looking to the side, to the floor, as if to recall how it's done, or maybe seeing herself in her mind from all that time ago, maybe she can see her former selves, and then begins. Slowly. Just beating on the goatskin first with her right hand, then left, then right and left, and both at the same time, *dap . . . dap . . . da dap, da dap, dap, dap, dap dap dap dap, dap dap dap dap, da dap da dap*, her eyes always on the floor as if reading invisible notes there, then whoosh, she shakes it vertically, as if it were a little baby in her hands, the way someone might enthusiastically lift a child before throwing her in the air, except she doesn't let go, just lifts the drum up, then pulls it fast down toward her lap a few times so that the ringlets tell their own story for a few moments, then she adds her own voice to it, a quiet, beautiful song in a language none of

216

us speak, but each of us feels deeply as we sit there listening in complete silence.

I don't know what it is exactly—the fact that she is so surprised, so happy with this gift, or that it brings back Iran like a wave rolling in, all the decisions and indecisions of the past rising around her, right there in that room, or the fact that here is someone who could do this for her—gifting her something that immediately connects her present-day self to all that she has been. He helps her sing. I think it is all of this, and my eyes well up.

Here is my friend, present for a love of her own choosing, living life on her own terms.

"Nobody can live your life, Ani," she told me once.

When I ask her later if she can translate the calligraphy on the skin of the drum, she says it is an old Hafiz poem, something about loving selflessly and that when you do, your love can reach up to the skies and everyone can hear it. It's what has happened right here this night—although Tim couldn't have known what the calligraphy said, his gesture and Sara's reaction have taken on a voice of their own and, as we witness, our hearts lift that voice further to the skies.

This is one of those evenings you never forget, when you know it marks someone and that it marks you, too, on the periphery of her story. It is Sara's evening, yet I sense it touching me unlike anything I have known in years. Here are two people whose lives have intersected in the most improbable way—Sara's long and winding journey all the way from Iran, and Tim's, the all-American quiet young man who's been to

217

war and back in more ways than one—here are these two thirty-somethings who did not rush into anything, who resist labeling a relationship and live what they create, who decided one day to build a shed and every weekend it gets taller and stronger and closer to being finished, from whose lips you don't hear proclamations, but you can see it in the way he grills and brings a plate to her lap, or when she speaks to him in the Persian he's learned, or when she tells me, "Sometimes I wonder, where has he learned how to do *that*!?" and we both laugh, all body, all hearts.

As we all sit there listening to Sara play and sing, the evening weaves itself into a language I had avoided, perhaps refused to listen to in years. But I hear it tonight. Love is a language people can only write together when they are ready, but also willing and unafraid to fail. Writing has always been my way of walking toward such language when I have recognized and claimed it as my own.

I HAVE A MOUTH

45

FOUR YEARS AFTER ISHAN and I divorce, I am having lunch with my mother and it just comes out. I have not planned it, but here I am telling her what happened to me in eighth grade in an alley one morning. Soon afterward, I tell her about my unconsummated marriage.

She looks shocked, that look on her face like she smells something bad. Like it's my fault.

I ask her why it's so shocking. "We never spoke about sex in school, in the family, in social circles, on TV when I grew up. Did you?"

"No," she says. "We didn't either."

"Those guys were harassing me nearly every day, for years. Did you notice something, did I ever talk about it?"

"No," she says, and she can only sit there thinking. I tell her how isolated I felt through all those years of harassment in Albania, through college, as the only Albanian who still knew nothing about dating. I tell her that I went all the way to Thailand because I believed someone loved me.

And I married someone I actually didn't trust. He had his own issues. We were inexperienced. "What are you worried about?" I ask her.

"I'm worried about when my daughter will find someone. Why she has this fate." She says this the way my father always says it. Final. Like that is the only way to exist and be happy in the world—with someone—as though every person is made to grow up and find a partner for life, that if you don't, by a specific time, before a certain expiration date, you're doomed. It reminds me of my aunt, my father's sister, who still ends her conversation with me on the phone with the words *me një fat të bardhë* (wishing you a good fate).

It's a typical line Albanians wish on single people, mostly on single women.

What about all the life I have already lived? How does she not see that my fate has been so good to me already? Yes, it would be great to have someone in my life. I want to be with someone long-term and witness his life, all of his life, for as long as I'm given the time to witness it and vice versa. I'm one of those people who wants that. But I don't need that to feel complete the way she seems to think I should. Another person doesn't make a home for me. I am already home with myself. But I don't tell her any of this. Instead, I tell her not to tell Dad. Or go ahead, I say, tell him. Doesn't matter.

She tells him that same night when I drop her home. We are all sitting in their living room.

"She must have made it up, her writer's imagination," is what my father says. I am right there. When I ask him which part

220

he thought I had made up, he says, "It's not possible for you to have been married so long and never had sex! What were you, psychologically ill? And how can you tell this to other people? Writing a book. This is not something to share."

It's why they call these things secrets. Secrets families live with. What did you call it? "Psychological illness." What would happen if I took your fears and painted them all over town? I'm back to the day I tried to kill myself. My mother is telling me to stay in the bedroom so my parents' friends won't find out. Stay in the bedroom. Stay in the bedroom. I'm not staying in the damn bedroom. Didn't then and never will.

"You're lonely," Jean tells me at a session soon after this encounter with my parents. "What does it feel like?"

"Like I'm suspended in space, out in the universe, just me, detached from everything, no planets around, a black void, just me up there at this mouth, like a black hole, or like I'm about to knock on some invisible door of the cosmos but I know no one will hear so no one will let me in."

I have come to understand why my parents reacted that way. They couldn't process the information yet because they haven't had the time or space to make peace with it as I have. I know that my father's immediate reaction was to deny what he heard because he felt terrible, like he had failed to protect his only daughter, so instead of listening, he tried to reject what he heard. It was painful. And although I knew it wasn't their fault or mine, for the first time in my life I feel detached from my parents. As though they're only a vessel through which I came into this world but I'm ultimately alone in my experience. Not even they can help me. Can't be the parents I always needed. Can't understand where I come from. Can't see where I can go. Not yet. Not yet. And there is loneliness again. It's just me in front of something without form, in the face of the deep. It's so real it physically hurts.

"That's not all of who you are, you know," Jean continues. "We have all these sides of us: jealous, lonely, happy, sad, angry. Each one is who we are, but that's not all we are."

She makes sense. Because when I'm in that space, feeling loneliness and nothing else, it is so hard to think of feeling any other way. So hard to believe that it might be possible to not feel this way. If I could pinpoint utter loss, it would be this—a complete detachment and isolation from the world. This and maybe the only other time I can think of is when I had to put Petey down. Not the aftermath of the injection—that was the most peaceful part of having to say goodbye to him—but the finding out that he was going to die. Realizing that I had to let him go and learning to do just that. Nobody tells you that letting go is something that needs to be learned. I'm glad a dog taught me that.

46

One night, about a year and a half after Jai and I start dating, I decide to tell him: "I can't continue this way. I want more. I can't keep spending the night at your place and living out of a bag every day."

I have lost a sense of home. My own apartment doesn't feel like my place anymore. His apartment isn't mine either, though I have a key to it. We won't move in together because he doesn't know where he'll go when his daughter graduates high school.

"I want to have that option," he says. "All my life I've had to live here to be closer to the kids, but when she leaves, I can finally go anywhere."

"Okay, nobody is forcing you to stay. And we don't know if we'll still be together then, but if we are, I could go with you." I still have so much hope.

"No. I'm not going to let you do that. I can't let you do that. You have a responsibility to your parents. They've sacrificed everything for you. You can't just leave them. You need to be near them. I am not going to have you regretting moving away from them when the time comes that they will need you. I'm not going to be responsible for that."

"So you get to decide what I want to do about my parents?" I ask him, frustrated. "Even if they're all right with it? Because I know they would be. They want me to be happy first."

"Yes. I am making it my decision."

And that is it. I return the key.

"You don't have to do that now," he says.

"I know," I say. "I want to."

I go back to my place and finally start to clean Ishan's stuff out of the attic.

It is spring break, just in time for spring cleaning. I am finally getting Ishan's stuff out of my apartment. It has been four years

223

since he moved away to try farming in California and had no place, family, or friends with whom to store his stuff. I thought it would be for a year, and I had the extra space, but it has been several years now. I finally write to tell him I am shipping what he wants and donating the rest.

I have often done this, hold and hold until I can't anymore and one day I'm done. I am done taking care of Ishan. In fact, I realize that I am done taking care of Ishan because I am ready to be done waiting around for Jai.

I put together a huge backpack, fill it with Ishan's hiking gear, shoes, torch, first aid kit, and Smartwool clothes. I ship it to him and he pays for it. I take all the books from the shelves that I'm not attached to and donate them at the Goodwill in town. About two hundred books. Eight thirty-gallon garbage bags of clothes, curtains, towels, Ishan's shoes that couldn't be shipped off. Among all the stuff, I find this tiny envelope with passport pictures of Ishan through the ages. He looks like a different boy, and then a different young man, through all of them.

What is his life like now? Is he happy and can he hold on to that happiness? As he works in those fields walking cows or butchering chickens, what does he care about the most? Has he found someone that is good to him? Is he good to her? I hope that he's found someone. I have always felt gratitude that he chose to end the marriage when he did. I know it couldn't have been easy. I hope he did it to save his life. I know he's been saving his life every day since then. Maybe he realized then that he also needed to save mine. No. I saved mine, but

224

it was as though he decided to bring me to the water, and then I dared to swim.

For most of my life I have lived like a flower grown in a shop— there to be watched, looked at, wondered about, never free outdoors in the sun.

You are born a girl in this world and you're already measured with a different stick.

You are born a girl in Albania in the late seventies and you learn to not rock the boat. When you do, God's own wrath descends upon you with the might of people who'll shout a thousand words a minute to let you know you were wrong to ever open your mouth.

You learn that when someone dictates how you should behave, you shouldn't be surprised when, after you do exactly what they told you to do, they blame you—here is where being yourself is wrong already. Here is where your existence irks someone to death. Here is where you try your best to disappear so they won't see you, so they'll lay off your back. You learn this from your parents who've learned it from everyone around them.

Here is where you were raped on the street at twelve while going to school one morning.

You tell no one because you're scared of what it meant and could mean once you tell it. Would it grow and suffocate you and your whole family? You keep it like a seed somewhere within.

Except one day it sprouts. At forty, you will read the prose you've written about it to a large audience. Among friends and other Americans in the audience, there are several Albanians.

There have never been any Albanians at any of your readings before. You tell them you are nervous but, when you read, you are all voice. You read about the language you grew up around and how it betrayed you. How you shed that language the moment you stepped into another country as an eighteen-year-old immigrant. You read the scene of the rape. And you deliver it unflinchingly, the whole audience rapt, gasping, then loudly applauding you at the end.

If beginning to write in English, nearly twenty years ago, was an arrival and an entrance, reading your work in front of this audience—even though not in your mother tongue, even though some of them are listening to you read about their world in a foreign tongue—resists definition. It's just who you are—the writer, driven by a desire to be honest with her readers. The language you use—an inner compass to navigate how you want to create meaning. And you follow it, as always, sensitively, courageously.

It is a great reading. You know it. So does everyone else. For the first time, you don't need someone to confirm this for you.

For the first time, you've spoken, perhaps unsettled a listener, and some Albanians in the audience are moved. They come up to say so afterward. And yet someone tries to choke the story that you told. An Albanian journalist writes about the event in a newspaper, describing your rape in her own words, perhaps

On the cross-section figure of a tree trunk
you can make out her first year of growth.
If the space between tree rings is wide,
it indicates a rainy season.
If it's narrow, the season was dry.
You can even tell when she was scarred
from forest fire and how she kept growing.
And there's an old wound
that began to change her face.

in an attempt to translate it, adding details that never happened, using quotation marks as though it is your story.

You are raped again. This time by a woman. This time right through your mother tongue.

Let's say her mistakes weren't intentional. But that is not the point.

When an Albanian friend who reads the article asks you if the story is true, you tell her, yes, I was raped, and this is what actually happened.

"What a shame he didn't use his penis," she says, laughing, trying to make a joke, meaning that then it would have counted, and you laugh with her briefly, though what is this feeling of being choked again, so you say: "It doesn't matter if he used his penis or his hand, he forced himself on me. I was twelve, I didn't know him, I didn't want any of what he did to me. It was rape."

She shuts up, her eyes ablaze, and says nothing.

You don't need her to say anything. You don't need her apology or the absence of an apology. Her response, even this silence, doesn't matter to you. All that matters is that you spoke your mind.

What if you buy the flower in the shop and plant her in the field? Will the flower remember having lived in captivity? When she's warmed in the sun, or swaying in the breeze, or drenched in the rain, will she taste freedom for however long she has left to live?

I don't know. But I have to try so that the world will one day fill with people planting flowers where they belong, under the sun. So that each time a girl is born, she is born free.

47

I have been speaking my mind.

Out with Jai and some friends one night, when he tries to offer me advice, I tell him I don't need him to teach me another lesson. I just need a friend.

At work, when someone tries to embellish my statements, I tell her I don't want her to embellish the things she thinks I'm thinking.

When my brother makes fun of me again, I call him out. Where is it coming from? We're not kids anymore.

When my boss offers me a new contract for the job I already have, I refuse it and write up a proposal for a new position I create. It doesn't work, but that's fine. Later, she'll come back with a better proposal.

When my landlord keeps working on the roof outside my living room window without scheduling it with me first, I tell him it's inappropriate. He needs to text or call me before he gets up here.

My parents, too—they keep asking me why I'm still friends with Jai even though we're not dating anymore. I tell them I can choose who remains my friend and who doesn't and that's all.

The insurance company presents me with a valuation report after I total my car but it's insufficient. I present my own re-evaluation and supporting materials and get an additional $1,700 on top of what they first quoted me.

When I visit six different dealerships to purchase a lease on a new car, I do it by myself.

No dad, no brother, no male friend to do the talking for me.
When I share this with Jean, she asks me what I need.

"More clarity," I reply. "To assert what I already know."

"You want to tell the truth, right? What is your truth?"

I think for a while. Language often feels unavailable to me
when she asks something so simple; the answer is hard to accept,
and therefore hardest to articulate.

"This isn't good enough for me," I finally say. "I want to
matter. That's what I want the most. That's what I no longer
feel with Jai, what I haven't felt enough of with him."

Jean asks me to think of an image for how I feel at this very
moment. What comes to me is a red lily in a field. A single
flaming lily.

"You mean you're alone?" Jean asks.

"No, it's not that. It's not about being solitary. It's that the
lily is right there, the color is an announcement of its presence."

"You are asserting your presence?" she wants to confirm.
"Don't let me put words in your mouth."

"You're not putting words in my mouth. That's exactly it," I
say. "Not alone. Very comfortable actually being out there, in
my environment, unique, fitting in."

Every time I leave Jean's office, which is nearly always at night,
I back my car out of her driveway, which is paved in small tiles
and not exactly parallel to a wall on my right, and sometimes
I have to put the car back into drive and realign my car so that
I won't hit the wall. If I back up following the alignment of the
tiles, I will hit the wall. If I align my car with the wall and look

229

at the tiles, their arrangement creates the illusion that I am not backing up straight. I have to trust that both the wall and my steering wheel aren't lying. On nights when I know we have done the best work, I am able to back up smoothly in one go, without even looking at the wall to keep the car straight. Other times, I have to reverse, drive, reverse, drive, reverse again. I've always thought the driveway has given me its own lessons on how important it is to trust myself.

ATDHE: HOME

48

MY GRANDMOTHER MEROPI passed away on February 17, 2001, at the age of ninety-six. When she was on her deathbed, my uncle says she kept repeating the phrase, *Jezu Krishti është i biri i Perëndisë* (Jesus Christ is the Son of God).

This petite ninety-six-year-old woman, whose eyesight had gone in the last few months of her life, was saving part of her bread every morning to feed the birds on the balcony, leaning a little too far over the railing because she couldn't see very well. I can see her almost flying off, arms outstretched the way she'd have them when she prayed, so many times, back in my childhood when we lived together. I would wake up in the middle of the night and there she was, flat on the floor, whispering prayers. She'd get up and lift her arms, then bow down and lie flat again, then up, three or four or five times. Always facing north. And me facing her. I have never been so dedicated.

My uncle doesn't know why my grandma said those words on her deathbed. Neither does my father, though I have never asked either of them directly. But it strikes me that even a woman of

231

such strong faith felt she had to say this at the time of her last breath. I wonder if she said those words because she wanted so badly to arrive in heaven. That if God heard her last words, he would know how devout she was and he would take her in.

Maybe I'm wrong, right, Grandma? You really believed it. But why would you say those words on your deathbed, blind as a bat. Were you doubting them? Fine. I will believe that that was all the home you needed to arrive at. That deep acceptance—call it acceptance, call it surrender, call it knowing. Knowing "it is finished" and being okay with that.

All I know right now is that home for me cannot be anything depicted in any book, cannot be taken from a dream. Another person cannot be my home. And in realizing all this I'm left with myself. My body. My heart beating. My blood. My soul. My aloneness. These are my only home. This moment. My presence.

Home is anywhere I stop to think about believing. There are no mistakes. Only choices.

A long day of childhood in which you play, get bruised, get up and play again till you sit on the sidewalk waiting for your best friend to have had enough of the game and you fall asleep, arms crossed, head on your knees.

I drive my prayers home every time I think of how much I love myself. It is a little like going up the stairs in a house after all the guests have left, satisfied with everything, and the dishes are somehow all done, and the evening is all mine, and all the tomorrows can wait.

Home. There is no word in Albanian for it, though some will translate it as *shtëpi*, which is the word for *house*, denoting the edifice, the place one dwells in physically. Yet there is a word in Albanian that I think comes closest to the English meaning of *home* and maybe surpasses what this English word means to me. *Atdhe* is the Albanian word for the place where we are born and our ancestors lived. Atdhe is the permanent dwelling of a people. It's where something can be born and mature. And more literally, it's the earth of our fathers.

Hello, mother—snail
   crossing a sidewalk
always there before I
   take my next step,
but the green grass,
   that is my father
and on the last day,
   he'll cover me.

I arrive in atdhe when I open my palm and let everything go, yet I feel surrounded by all I have loved and all I have lost. Petey is here. My grandmother is here. My childhood is here. Tiranë is here. Everyone I have loved is here. God is here. And I am God.

When I am still a teenager, I have a dream in which I'm looking out from my balcony, toward the sky, when the clouds open up theater-curtain-style onto a gigantic stage to reveal the heavens, paradise, life after death, God's place, although there is no God or beautiful wild animals or people, only golden streets and golden mansions. Everything is glistening, glowing, bejeweled under a perfectly blue sky. I think I have an orgasm just looking at it all. It feels, in the dream, like this view reveals to me that paradise-after-death is real, except when I wake up, I have the sudden realization that the dream isn't so special anymore. That I have seen this view before. It looks like the illustrations in Arthur S. Maxwell's *The Bible Story* series that foreign missionaries from America have brought us. Clearly my dream is a manifestation of, or response to, what I have been looking at in my waking hours. I am so disappointed.

But I think of this now, this "destination," this place where all who believe in a heaven want to go, and realize that I'm always worried about death. I can't understand why everything has to die. There's so much beauty here in knowing one another, each other's strengths and losses, witnessing all of that. I don't understand why that gift of witnessing has to end. Something so meaningful as loving someone, a parent, a child, a friend, a dog, a house, a river, a rock—having to never see them again. Why were we given all this?

"Where is your grandmother?" Jean asks me when we are talking about this fear of death.

"She's dead."

"Is she gone?" she asks again, without forming another question to clarify, so that it hits me as I think about it, that no, not really, she hasn't gone anywhere except maybe she's inside me?

"There's this old saying, I forget from where," she says. "Old friends will come and go, but the dead are always with us."

I cry because I have known the same with Petey. And I realize that crying is also a way my body tells me it has recognized and received a truth.

The more I question death, the further from answers I get. But deep down I have this strong sense that my questioning has something to do with home. As though home is the opposite of death and once I reach it, or have a better grasp of what it is, I will no longer be afraid to die, or to lose it all, because there is

234

no loss. Only a transition. Another form of experiencing home. Maybe. I will never stop thinking this through.

49

In the Andes, there is a group of people who speak the Aymara language and think of time very differently from the rest of us. For the Aymara people, the future, *qhipa pacha/timpu*, translates as *back* or *behind time*, and the past, *nayra pacha/timpu*, as *front time*, meaning that the past always sits in front of us because we think about where we come from, what we have done. But the future is behind us, unknown to us, something we can't foresee.

"All right, I should go," Jai says one morning, trying to get out of bed. It's been hard for both of us to walk away.

I walk him to the living room and we stand together for a moment. He puts his arms around me, but soon he kisses my neck and I'm kissing his, our heads dancing very slowly forehead to forehead, our hands begin to travel like train cars without locomotives, they go anywhere. Behind me, on the wall, I'm aware of Gustav Klimt's *The Kiss* hanging, perhaps eyeing us, but I don't fall to my knees. I'm standing in the middle of the living room with him standing before me, the morning light stunned around us. For an eternal moment, we're the only gods alive in the world. He pulls my sleeping shirt down and my right breast rises out. He kisses it or tries to gulp it or both. Then he pulls my shirt up but doesn't take it off and bends to nibble on my left nipple as I bite his shoulder, then his chest, and start to lift his shirt though I don't take it off either. He moves his hands to unzip his pants, but his hands don't know how to follow through and we're breathing now like trains down a valley. I unzip him and as I lower his pants my mouth draws a perfect invisible line vertically down to the source of what made him come here last night, and as the rest of me follows my mouth, he pulls my shirt over my head. I rise again and kiss him on the mouth, then I lower my own pants. They fall on the floor with my underwear—prayers that go nowhere. He leads me back to the bedroom where our bodies swoop and swirl, the way his mouth suddenly falls right between my legs and then rises into my own mouth. We are too good at this.

Sometimes you just have sex because it's powerful to feel the other person experiencing power in the process of having his desires met—he's aroused by you at first and then is allowed to feast on you. It's powerful to feed someone, to control his hunger. I do not like this side of me. There is no heart in it. The heart is a winged little thing that has waited and waited for love. I devour it mindlessly the moment I decide I will arouse him.

What about him? Why has he come back this time? What else does he want from me?

Why doesn't he admit it? He is addicted to watching me get turned on under his touch, as his breath traverses my neck, his grip on my side, on all of my insides.

The truth is simpler than all that. We both love sex. And in knowing this, I allow him whatever he wants—the more he gets what he wants, the more he gives back. I like watching him surrender. I have become someone who desires to see it, to watch the complete surrender of another.

Sometimes, you just have the kind of sex where you see yourself pulling all the strings and the sex morphs endlessly, all shape and no language. Sometimes you do it, knowing too well, for the last time.

"I'm not going to have sex with you anymore," I tell Jai one night when we are smoking cigars on the patio of his cottage on the Cape. "I don't want a part-time relationship. I'm serious this time."

"I know you're not going to," he says. "I can see it in your eyes."

"Good," I say, taking a drag, not blinking.

"Look at your cigar burning perfectly, you haven't had to relight it or anything."

"Confidence," I say, surprised that I answer back so quickly with that word, and laugh. I think of Pura Lopez Colome, who I met in Slovenia at a poetry festival, who gave me these two cigars. I told her I would have them with "a good friend of mine."

"Strive to be happy, Ani," she said in parting. I am, strangely enough, feeling happy at this very moment, making this decision.

We sleep in separate beds that night. As I try to fall asleep, I feel as though I am being watched by a black-haired woman looking at me from outside a window frame, which is outside a window frame, outside a window frame, and on and on. She seems to watch me from far away. Her face is distorted; she looks as though she can't make up her mind whether she wants to scare or warn me about something. Who is she? Buried

Rozafa? Some ancestor? Just my imagination? I make my mind's eye turn and look at her straight on, and the more I stare, the closer she appears, one window frame disappearing at a time until her face grows larger into a dark shadow, the whole night encircling me. As I begin to feel the darkness overtake me, I tell it to fuck the hell off, and it dissolves like incense smoke and I finally fall asleep.

In childhood, when I capture life in the palm of my hand, looking at those insects and grass inside the box of glass, I am playing creator. Now in adulthood, I have seen the life of many relationships and have learned which connections to value. Now I am that creator, shaping stories. Now is when I breathe. When I know what I want, and even when I know that, I don't know what exactly I want.

50

In all the years since the divorce, I have kept in touch with Ishan. We've become friends who check in with one another and encourage each other on whatever new thing is happening next in our lives. He updates me on the women he keeps falling for, the beautiful, playful tunes he comes up with on his guitar, the

They have survived one another.
The earth holds them the way it holds
children: gladly and curiously affected.

house he rents and decorates—he seems more at peace. But he still annoys me sometimes, like when he asks who I'm taking to the PEN America Literary Awards ceremony.

"My mother."

"What are you doing that for?" he asks. "How's anyone supposed to introduce himself to you with her hanging around like a cold?"

"Like a cold?! My mother?!" I'm a little shocked, upset that he still holds a grudge against her, my hands beginning to sweat already, but I continue: "If anyone won't meet me because my mother is around, then I'm not interested in meeting them either."

I know what you're thinking. Look at Ani, the empowered woman who reclaims her body. But I don't know who that is. To me, that's as much a cultural construct as the bombshell of the sixties. When I look back at choices I have made, I recognize myself as a curious, creative being who sometimes cannot wait to start something, a woman who gives herself space and several chances to figure things out, takes risks and forgives herself, allowing herself all the time she needs in the process. I have always done so. I don't have a name for who I am, because I love all the selves within, most of all the girl who evaded the streets of her youth and knew those little fists inside her pockets would one day write the story she held in, until she alone knew how to tell it. Some men have called me *stubborn*. Some women—*such a nice girl*. Neither label defines me.

How strange to be here, eight years after Ishan tells me he's leaving, five after Ben and I break up, one year after I say goodbye to Jai, never to chase after him again. Maybe we'll always be friends, Ishan and I. Jai and I. Maybe we'll lose these friendships again. I don't know what will happen. I know I loved both of these men and I have continued to love again; often, I have loved so much in the years I have been single to know that love is a gift, not a quest.

Here, everything is an instant of tension—
shapes continuously touching, perching
so that one's weight never cancels the other's.

I decide to travel alone to Ireland, a place I have never been but always wanted to see, a place where I know no one.

In Dublin, I take the bus to a small town on the southwest coast purely for the reason that I feel drawn there. On the first day of my arrival, I walk as far on Main Street as there are shops; just as I am about to return, I tell myself to take a few more steps, to see a little farther.

I hope I always choose a little farther over seeing enough.

I stumble upon a pottery shop and meet the potter inside, a man whose age I can't pin to a number but whose hair is almost all white. He has the body, gaze, and smile of Leonard Cohen. He turns from the window he is looking out of and says hello and introduces himself. It will be over four hours before I will leave his place. From the moment we start talking, there is something that we are both aware of—we can't stop talking about our pasts, how we have made our way and life in another land. He is originally from Germany, where he left his family in his youth. He gave his whole life to art, he says, to never be bound by anyone but his desire to create.

"You need to figure out a way to do the same," he tells me, and although that reminds me of Jai telling me what I should do, I continue to listen and sit on a stool next to him because I am interested in seeing more of the whole person, not define him by one thing he says that I don't agree with. Before too long, we are both crying.

"Can you believe this?" he asks. "You can't have come from Albania, married an Indian, moved to the U.S., then come to Ireland, all the way here into my shop, to cry with me. This doesn't happen often."

I agree. But I also know what this is—two strangers who have allowed themselves to be seen by the other because we have both the fortune and the misfortune to probably never meet again.

"Come have coffee, or tea with me, in my house," he offers, looking me straight in the eyes, which lets me know he wants to spend more time talking, that Jean gaze that says I can trust this person.

I accept. I am forty-one years old, in a country where I know no one, where I have arrived of my own planning and choosing, when I know I can trust myself, and that if I'm in trouble, I will get myself out of it.

I follow him down the stairs from his shop through a small black door into an entirely different world that seems to merge all my pasts and all the futures I cannot know of yet.

His house is half art gallery and half shrine, decorated meticulously with sculptures and paintings from Hindu gods to Thai Buddha portraits and statues, to works by Horst Antes and Norbert Rumpke, art pieces that resist definition and seem to be in conversation with one another. Incense is burning and somewhere between its scent and being suddenly confronted with so many faces that seem to stare at me, I am stunned. Although

I take that back—none of them stare at me, but they frighten me, even as they look in their own directions and have their own presence. I had not expected to see so many Hindu gods in Ireland. Why is India following me here? I think to myself.

I have not thought of the possibility that someone, anyone out there could have an interest in these things, or the possibility that someone with these interests would build his home in this remote village at the edge of western Europe.

We sit down at his kitchen table. He makes me toast with butter and Swiss cheese and a cup of tea, which he pours into one of the cobalt blue mugs he has made.

We talk the whole time with the exception of a few moments when, through the camera, he sees customers enter his shop and needs to go upstairs to tend to them.

"Feel free to look around," he says. "Go sit in that area," pointing to another room. "See how you like it there. I want you to get all the energy in by yourself."

It is strange. All this trust and how he speaks to me. How does he know I won't steal something? What is it that makes me not take out my cell phone to photograph this fascinating world I have stepped into?

At some point I decide it is time for me to leave and he says okay, "but you should come back around seven, we can take a walk and exchange our minds more, deepen our friendship."

Okay, I say, knowing I won't go back.

And I don't.

When I think about my decision to not return, I feel a sense of pride that I allowed myself the space to meet and get to know someone, then listened to my body when I considered whether to go back to see him again.

On my way out of the shop, he wraps a new mug in newspaper and gives it to me.

One of the pieces in his home that I won't forget is a lithograph by Horst Antes, an artist unknown to me till that day. It is a figure of an androgynous-looking person with their right hand prying open a vulva-like slit in their chest, an erect penis sticking out just below it. It is, to me, a portrait of someone who puts their whole hand inside the wound. In fact, wound and pleasure are one, and this man I have just met seems to reflect both. Or maybe he simply reflects what my life has embodied till now. I think that's why we both cry.

At the time, I tell him how much the Antes lithograph reminds me of Sheela-na-gig, the Irish goddess of fertility. But he doesn't know anything about Sheela-na-gig and neither do other people in Ireland or the U.S. when I ask them.

If there's anything you can learn from a river, from the joy of a dog let off the leash,

it's this: you're never not your longing.

There are at least one hundred stone-carved sculptures of Sheela-na-gig in Ireland, where they're most predominantly found, although one finds them also in England, Scotland, Wales, France, and Spain. It's a twelfth-century phenomenon. Sheela-na-gig is the figure of a typically naked woman sitting with her legs wide open, holding on to or holding open an exaggerated vulva, her inner core willingly exposed. Some Sheelas look menacing, are made to resemble grotesques and placed

243

like them, like gargoyles, high up on top of church walls, some say to ward off evil, some to warn against lust and sins of the flesh. Some call her a hag, a witch, some don't know what to make of her.

I don't know what early Christians were thinking of, displaying Sheelas on church walls. I go to see one in Dublin, at Malahide Castle, on one of the walls of an abbey ruin. It is difficult to make out because the carving is worn and the abbey is surrounded by a fence you aren't allowed to trespass. I take a few moments and sit right across from her, sipping a cup of coffee while everyone and their children and dogs walk past me, none of them looking in the direction I am. I think about Rozafa, buried alive on the wall of her own house, and Sheela, placed here on the wall of a church. One left a breast, an arm, a leg, and an eye out for her child. The other openly points to her most inner part.

Many say that Sheela-na-gig is a symbol of fertility, a goddess through which all of life starts. I like that, although I like better what she means to me, the ordinary woman so at ease with her own body and mind that she is not ashamed or afraid when she puts her hand where she can feel herself most open, open like a flower, like soft earth after rain, pliable, malleable, when one thing leans toward another and transforms itself along. She is the ouroboros, at once an entrance and an exit.

What's the meaning of a figure like this reaching us from a thousand years ago? Maybe there is no meaning. We are not meant to understand. We are meant to look. We are meant to *not* look away. Hers is the way a woman knows herself. *Take a good look*, she says. *I have a mouth, and I love that, and how, and what, it makes me feel. You have one, too.*

I ask a bartender out. I ask my eye doctor out. Apparently, I have balls when I want them.

In the last couple of years, I have dated no one. I didn't feel like I needed to, nor did I want to. I knew that if I wanted to, I would.

But I would be lying if I said I hate being single. I love it. It is the opposite feeling I had when traveling to India for the first time, of being a tiny drop of mercury, completely detached from everyone yet so in need of attachment. Since those fifteen days in Ireland, I have felt more certain on my own two feet, more clear in my truths, reaching inside myself on my own to center and ground myself while navigating situations, drawing boundaries with other people where I need to speak up for myself.

My friends Sara and Tim have two little boys now, and my brother and sister-in-law the most fearless, confident six-year-old girl I have ever met. I'm not a mother, but in my own ways I mother my friendships as well as my parents and hope to do that for a long time.

My hands still sweat. I still find it difficult to articulate myself in public.

But I am at home on the page. And it is often on the page where my parents and I speak most openly to one another when we write emails and texts.

Years earlier, Jai asked me if I would change anything about my life if I could go back. I told him no.

"Wouldn't you want to not have married Ishan, not go through the years of being harassed and assaulted?"

I tell him no again. Has he forgotten that I married Ishan because I wanted to? Has he not understood that I loved him? Why would I want to change that?

"That's sad to me. Wouldn't you want a world where you would not be silenced for being a girl?"

"Of course I do. But I would absolutely not want it at the expense of erasing any of my experiences."

Life is longer and more spacious than the sum of the people we love and hurt from.

When a star dies, it becomes its burning. It cannot go back to adjust its shine. Why would it need to? All that ever matters is that it was a star. It shone its light. I was a quiet girl and an even quieter teenager. This allowed me to listen better in adulthood. And listening has allowed me to welcome and lean hard toward the certainty of my own burning.

In childhood, my mother tucks me in for a nap in the afternoons. The window in the bedroom looks out to the Lana River, lined with poplars. Lying down on the bed, I can only see their heads. They are like a row of old aunties overlooking my small little world. Looking in. Whereas I am not even looking out. I don't need to. They are always there.

I fall asleep watching leaves and branches sway left to right, right to left. Maybe this is how I learn to look people in the face. But for the longest time, I become afraid to do even this one thing I am good at.

More than three decades later, lying on the couch in my living room in Framingham, Massachusetts, I stumble upon explore.org, and open up a window that streams live video of animals in the wild, in Kenya. No one plans it, but here I am watching a lush green field, a giraffe in the middle, grazing, eye-level, on some trees. It is the first time I see a window as a mirror. I am right here. I am the giraffe.

The giraffe in the window stands there unaware that I am watching, eats very slowly, unbothered by the joy of hippos splashing in the water nearby. She is in her element, aware of her surroundings and unafraid. Present, but not needing to announce her presence. One with everything, yet fully on her own. She belongs and everything around her seems to fit and complement her presence. Food is all around her. She eats slowly, and when she moves, she moves even more slowly. Sometimes she goes out, then back into the frame of the camera, out, then back in, to the same rhythm of her jaws chewing earlier, or that of the poplar leaves and branches swaying in my childhood, and then moves on, the way a whole world and its people do when turning the last page of a book.

I think of Jean's words—"Could you have predicted this?"— about the night Ben and I first had sex. I think of what it was like with Jai, of the first time I came and cried with this man. My cry was a release for instantly recognizing how much I desired that moment in time with this specific person. How I could see and feel that he desired the same.

When my legs parted that December night in the car I was driving, before I met Jean, before Ishan moved out, before I could tell Ben, Jai, or my parents about what had happened to me at twelve and how I stayed in an unconsummated relationship for six years, I didn't know then what my body was telling me. It was telling me it had its own voice, its own language, and in that language it was saying, *Trust me*. It was saying, *You can trust this body with men, with the whole world, if and when you want to. The only unconditional love is the love of the body—how you listen to it, how it listens right back.*

EPILOGUE

I TURN MYSELF ON MY BACK, remove the bed covers, and take off my shirt. My breasts are already awake, waiting like little birds to be fed and my hands feed them as I run over them, under, pulling on one nipple, pulling on both. Unlike so many things in my life I have arrived at late, I have always mothered my desire.

Earlier, I took off my clothes to get in the shower. I'm a little older than my mother was the day she must have gone out to get groceries and came back to find me folding and putting away her clothes. I must have been five or six, maybe seven, the same age I remember being when all my life happened to me. I folded her shirts and with each fold she was right there. Her scent—sweet-wet earth, crushed rose and peony petals, tar cloud, talcum powder though she never wore any—was the scent of hard work and an entirely unselfconscious young woman who made sure she was present for everyone else: husband, two children, a mother-in-law, and a ten- or twelve-hour shift.

Standing in front of the mirror in my bathroom, lifting my arms to pull off my shirt, I notice for the first time that my armpits smell like my mother's did so many years ago. I smell them again the way you return to hug a friend you know you won't see for a while. I tell the mother in my memory: "I'll always remember you like this—forever youthful—alive in me."

I have never seen my parents have sex. I have never asked my mother if she's ever enjoyed it. Now, under the covers, I remember the night a man rolled over to kiss me and stopped and breathed in so deeply when face-to-face with my right armpit—I knew the animal in him. And it's this same animal of my body I'm here with tonight. I don't have to do anything more than pull on these red mouths for all the little mouths across my body to tell me *yes*. *Yes*, says my navel and twitches when I press on one of these birds; I think she smiles. *Yes* escapes my mouth and hovers over me like a firefly. *Yes*, behind my neck and under my ears, and deep within, a louder pulse, or maybe the temperature of my own blood answers back saying *yes*, *yes*, and somewhere deeper where I don't even need to locate it because it is so far inside me it's already the center of the universe, I feel a lift-off, and the entire ride I'm an explosion of *yes*, *yes*, *yes* stars, my body a mirror reflecting only light. I breathe.

My mother says that I talked to the leaves on the trees long before I started speaking. She would take me out on long strolls near the University of Tiranë under willow and poplar trees. I don't know if this is my origin story of loving language and words. I know that it's my origin of wanting to connect with the outside world. Like any child who hasn't yet begun to speak, the colors of the leaves and their quivering must have moved me. We respond to what is alive and seeking to communicate with us and we communicate in return. This is also why I choose to translate the kind of texts that most speak to me, where language is alive, when words on the page make me think and rethink about what the author is saying, and what the author allows me to figure out for myself.

For centuries, before borders were established, Greeks lived in Albania and Albanians lived in Greece. After my mother's mother, Grandma Garufo, an ethnic Greek woman from the village of Lefterohor, leaves her family home and mother tongue to marry my grandfather, Dhimitri, she listens secretly to Greek songs on the radio. These are the songs she grew up with, in the language she identifies with, but being a minority in Communist Albania means she has to hide the fact that she longed to hear her mother tongue. Imagine having no freedom of speech and no freedom to connect to what feels alive in you. Grandma Garufo cleans the house, then stands by the radio from time to time to listen in low volume to songs from a Greek radio station that the town of Korçë picks up in the 1950s.

"What does the song say?" my then ten-year-old mother asks her, begging to learn the language.

"Shh, it's not for you," my grandmother responds, because they are love songs.

Today, some seventy years later, on another continent, in Worcester, MA, my mother meets an Albanian immigrant who used to live in the house next door to Grandma Garufo, whose family was very close to my grandparents' family. He has suffered a stroke and doesn't remember a lot of things, but he remembers my grandmother's name. He goes to another room and comes back with a notebook.

"These are all Greek love songs that Garufo translated for me when I would ask her," he says, handing the notebook to my mother.

He has kept them all these years and brought them to America. The stroke did not erase his love for language; wherever we go, we carry language that moves us. We know it in our bodies when words needle like thread into our ears and hearts and a tingling is felt on the skin.

The Japanese believe in the spirit of words, that language has a soul, what they call *kotodama*. Language protects but it can also bring division, manipulation, and erasure in the hands of oppressors.

> The time will come when you, too, will speak,
> unrestrainedly like a church bell.

Words can have more than two extremes. Some say "grab them by the pussy" in order to degrade and suppress. But such language can also inspire and inflame.

"The Brain—is wider than the Sky—" says Emily Dickinson, but the body, where memory and language live, is an unobservable universe measured through the

> You will say everything
>   you want to say.
> It will mean exactly what
>   you want it to mean.
> And everyone will listen.
>   Everyone knows
> you are here.

sum of our emotions. I cry, I laugh, I get angry, I get sad, I'm disgusted, I'm silent, I'm afraid, I hate, I'm thrilled . . . To live is to allow ourselves to spin along all

> And when the time comes
>   for you to be quiet again
> you will be quiet like the
>   jasmine garden
> in the evening. And that
>   is all right.

human feelings on this ever-widening wheel and welcome each one.

Emotions are our teachers. They move us, for better or for worse, like language, and what moves us lives in our bodies and weaves the universe within. How lucky I have been to be able to share mine.

You have a mouth.

ACKNOWLEDGMENTS

To Joel Gardner—the first set of eyes on the very first draft of this book—thank you for hearing a voice in that early draft. Thank you for encouraging me to follow it.

Lidia Yuknavitch, Katherine Angel, Roxane Gay, Nina MacLaughlin, Kiese Laymon, Cheryl Strayed, Marguerite Duras, Garth Greenwell, Maggie Nelson—your books have taught me how to listen closely to the body and to language. They were my guides on the journey to find my words; rather, to allow language to find me. Thank you.

To my publisher, Ilan Stavans, and Shuchi Saraswat and Francisco Cantú—I'm immensely grateful that you picked my manuscript as the winner of the Restless Books Prize for New Immigrant Writing. I couldn't have dreamed of a better home for this book and a better prize to be recognized by. I am honored to have a new family among fellow immigrant writers I admire: Deepak Unnikrishnan, Grace Talusan, Priyanka Champaneri, Rajiv Mohabir, Meron Hadero, and others to come.

To editor Nathan Rostron—thank you for suggesting that I sprinkle more of my poetry throughout the book.

To my editor, Jennifer Alise Drew, who arrived at a crucial time and carried me all the way to the finish line, who understood this book deeply, trusted that I could follow her vision, and elevated the work to be its very best—thank you! You made this book sing. You made this book with me and you made it *ours*.

To Taylor Arnette—I never felt such pleasure working with a copyeditor, to watch you comb through the manuscript bringing more muscle to my prose.

To Lydia McOscar and everyone else at Restless Books I didn't work with directly, all the way to the book distribution personnel—thank you for your time, care, and all the patience that you give so that a book can find its readers.

To Alex Billington at Tetragon, London, who I imagine as part wizard and part photographer, working in a darkroom until the contours of each page come into view—what a thrill to see what you made. Thank you!

Similarly, Sarah Schulte—how you intuited my vision for the cover of this book! It is because you and Jen listened to me so deeply that this cover thrills me every time I look at it.

To the literary magazines *The Common*, *LitHub*, and *Plume*, who first published early versions of excerpts from this book—thank you.

To my first/best teachers ever in America: Deborah J. Leonard and Matthew Vollmer—you both sparked my imagination in those classes in the dining room of the White House so many years ago. You have done more to expand my understanding of what language can do than you will ever know. I love you dearly.

To my GrubStreet family, beginning with Alysia Abbott, who knew my book would one day be in the world before she read it, who taught me world-building and encouraged me onward—thank you. To Eve Bridburg and Kitty Pechet for supporting my writing when I most needed it. The Pauline Scheer fellowship made it possible that I could revise my book and learn so much in the process. To my Memoir Incubator classmates: Thu-Hằng Trân, Anne Crane, Theresa Okokon, Karen Kirsten, Virginia DeLuca, Linda Cutting, Rita Chang, and Anri Wheeler—thank you for inspiring me, for your insights, and your curiosity. To Rita and Anri in particular—thank you for persistently probing and cheering me onward.

To Matthew Vollmer, Mike Scalise, and Katherine Angel: You read this book at three crucial stages and I'm grateful for your feedback.

To my writer family: Jessica Moore, Stacy Mattingly, Dariel Suarez, Colwill Brown, Jonathan Escoffery, Yasmin Amelie, Tara Skurtu, Sonya Thayer, Mariya Gusev, Asya Graff, Colleen Doyle, Jordan Zandi, Rebecca Van Laer, Elizabeth Howard, Duy Doan, Rebekah Stout, Monica McCarter, Shubha Sunder, Hyeseung Song, Rachel Morgenstern-Clarren, Christopher Schmidt, Victoria Livingston, Valerie Hegarty, Laurel K. Dodge, James Lineberger, Scott Odom, Teresa Ballard, Lynzee, Jack Anders, Jenni Russell, Don Zirilli, and "Ishan"—each of you have fed my love for words at different stages of my life. I'm so grateful for knowing you and admire you deeply. Your work is so important and has inspired me to work harder with mine.

To Julia Gjika, Visar Zhiti, Luljeta Lleshanaku, and Xhevdet Bajraj—you have shown me how to write with a full heart. Thank you for entrusting me with your words through the years.

To my parents, my brother, Alison, and Leah, who inspire me daily and have taught me so much—I wanted to write this book to show the many ways I have loved. I'm so moved to discover that I wrote a book that shows how well I have been loved.

To "Ishan"—maybe you'll never read this book. What I wish is that you will write yours. I am grateful to both you and my parents for never asking me to show you what I'd written while working on it for years. It has meant the world to have this freedom and to have your faith in my abilities as a writer to tell my story.

To my grandmothers, Meropi and Garufo, and the women before them—you are always with me. I know you helped me write this book.

To Anita Hoffer—you have been at once a lighthouse and a compass. Thank you.

To my chosen family: Sara Khanzadi, Timothy Rudzinsky, Elijah Khanzadi Rudzinsky, Oliver Khanzadi Rudzinsky, Meridith Paterson, Kayıhan Turgutoğlu, Trudi and Ed Reinhart, Rita Chang and Mark DePuy, Deborah J. Leonard—I couldn't have finished this book without your friendship, enthusiasm, and support when I most needed it and the space you gave me so I could cocoon for weeks at a time to get it done.

To Millay Arts, where I first read out loud the prologue of this book to dear and talented friends I made there: Monika Burczyk, Calliope Nicholas, Jung Hae Chae, Joshua Solondz, Sarah Mangold, Ximena Velasco, Daniel Tejera. Thank you for the time and the beautiful space to work peacefully on the initial edits of this book.

To my Framingham High School family—Alison Courchesne, Veronica DeSouza, Sandra Strattman, Luisa Callahan, Cynthia Villanueva, everyone in the ESL and World Languages departments, Dr. Robert Tremblay, and the HR staff for their support in the process of publishing this book.

To my students, past and future, and particularly to the 2022–2023 students of Writing 3A and Social Studies and Literature 2A in room E204, the year this book was readying for publication—you have given me dreams. Thank you.

To David Gullette, Robert Pinsky, Louise Glück, Rosanna Warren—thank you for being the generous, kind mentors I needed.

To Caleb Slotnick—I admire your patience and kindness that have gone a long way toward making me feel held in the process of completing and letting go of this book. Thank you for being you.

To all my Albanian family and friends, current and to come, thank you for waiting. I have only been back to Albania once since leaving the country in 1996. I cannot wait to return many times and walk there again—this book is a start.

A NOTE ABOUT THE AUTHOR

Albanian-born writer Ani Gjika is the author and literary translator of eight books and chapbooks of poetry, among them *Bread on Running Waters* (Fenway Press, 2013), a finalist for both the 2011 Anthony Hecht Poetry Prize and 2011 May Sarton New Hampshire Book Prize. Gjika moved to the U.S. when she was eighteen, earning a BA in English at Atlantic Union College, an MA in English at Simmons University, and an MFA in poetry at Boston University. Her translation from the Albanian of *Negative Space* by Luljeta Lleshanaku was published in 2018 by Bloodaxe Books in the U.K., where it was Poetry Book Society's Recommended Translation and shortlisted for the International Griffin Poetry Prize. It was published in the same year by New Directions in the U.S., where it was a finalist for a PEN Award and Best Translated Book Award. Gjika is a recipient of awards and fellowships from the NEA, English PEN, the Robert Pinsky Global Fellowship, the 2019 Pauline Scheer Fellowship through GrubStreet's Memoir Incubator program, and, most recently, the 2021 Restless Books Prize for New Immigrant Writing for her memoir, *An Unruled Body*. Having taught creative writing at various universities in the U.S. and Thailand, Gjika currently teaches writing, social studies, and literature to English language learners at Framingham High School in Massachusetts.